Popular Antiques

Popular Antiques

edited by
Paul Atterbury

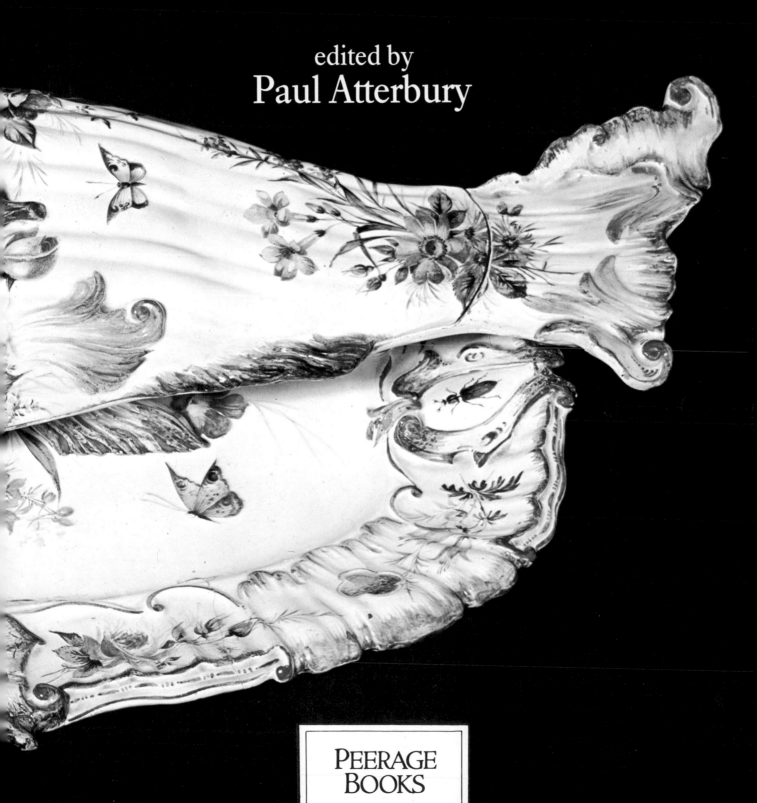

PEERAGE
BOOKS

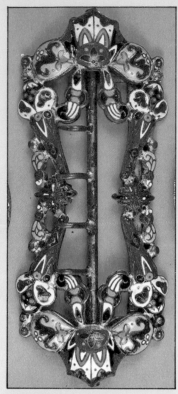

First published by
Octopus Books Limited
This edition published by
Peerage Books
59 Grosvenor Street
London W1

© 1977 Octopus Books Limited

ISBN 0 907408 00 1

Printed in Hong Kong

Contents

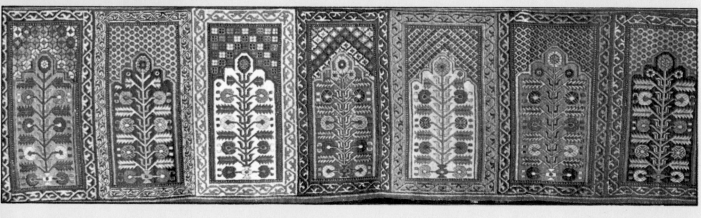

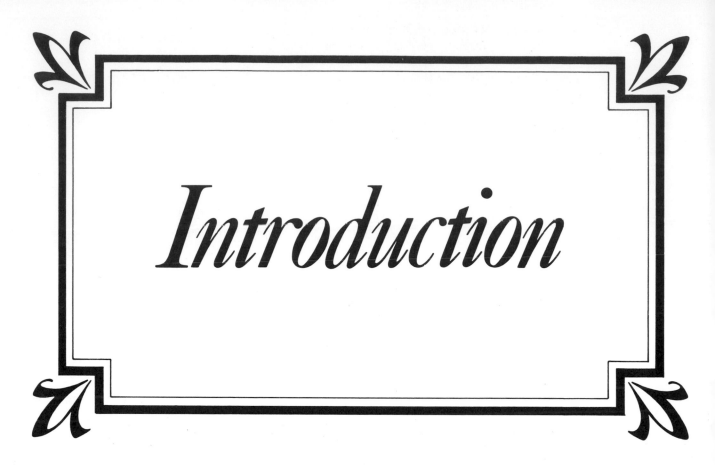

Introduction

What is a popular antique? Traditionally, to be an antique, or rather to be accepted as such by tax authorities, customs and similar bodies an object has to be at least one hundred years old. However, the more reactionary members of the antique trade tend to retain the long-established deadline of 1830 as the definition of an antique. This date has no historical significance, but it is a convenient barrier to hide behind. Safely entrenched and securely blinkered, the trade can disregard the whims of fashion, and avoid the problem of making value judgements about objects produced during the Victorian period and later. On the other hand, the more adventurous and stimulating members of the trade, and the majority of the collecting public set no arbitrary limit. For them, in the world of antiques, anything goes.

There is thus an immediate problem posed by the word 'popular'. Are popular antiques those objects that are commonly found only in museums, stately homes and the most important private collections? Or is a popular antique something which is readily available and widely collected by members of the public? This book attempts to answer both questions, and so is inevitably a compromise between traditional and contemporary definitions of an antique.

The solid, blue chip antiques of the eighteenth century and earlier are included in large numbers because no book of this type could leave them out. Such things may not be available to any but the richest collector, indeed some historic objects may be beyond price, but they are necessary as a background against which to judge all the more recent antiques. Any good collector,

A Louis XV Sèvres porcelain and gold rectangular snuff box, by Pierre Croissant, Paris 1744.

RIGHT *Derby figure of a boy about 1765.*

BELOW *Ash-framed chair with triangular rushed seat, English, mid-seventeenth century. This is a primitive version entirely handmade, of a type usually formed with lathe-turned members.*

whatever the field of interest, will always be familiar with the historical and artistic development of styles and have an appreciation of quality. These vital elements can either be instinctive or they can be learned; for a thorough awareness of the history of style and design can help to create an eye for quality. It is equally important for the collector to know that each age produced as much rubbish as fine things, and thus to avoid the classical error of confusing age with quality. Those who cower behind the 1830 deadline are suffering from this sort of confusion; they cling to a straw that they think is kept afloat by a notion of acceptable public taste, without realizing that public taste in fact left them high and dry years ago. They run the risk of simply vanishing like the dinosaur, and not, as they fear, of being drowned by a flood of novel and outrageous ideas and styles. They are simply old fashioned. For collecting and fashion exist hand in hand. The swings and roundabouts of fashion will throw up a succession of new fads, fancies and crazes.

Some will linger for a moment and then be swept away and forgotten; others will make their initial impact, and then will survive the onrushes of later passions to become an accepted part of the collecting establishment. So this book has also included examples of these new tastes that appeal to the collectors of the moment, not just because they are new but because they should be judged by the same criteria of style and quality as the well-established popular favourites. They are also included because they are popular in the sense of being available to the public. A book of this type should be an adequate reflection of what has become in recent years one of the most popular pastimes of the western world, namely antique collecting.

Collecting is exciting, and a gamble. You buy what you like, or what you have been directed to like by the prophets of fashion. You may end up richer, or poorer, but in either case you will end up wiser for the quickest way to learn about style and quality is to handle as many objects as possible. The collector of modest means and limited experience is likely to gain more pleasure, benefit and knowledge than the conservative who spends a lot of money on a conventionally acceptable object. On every level it is more worthwhile to buy a first class piece of Victorian or twentieth-century furniture than a tenth rate, over-restored eighteenth-century example. It often costs less too to pursue a new and unrecorded field, with the added bonus of the pleasure of breaking new ground. Many collectors today have been able to enjoy the antiques boom in terms of both money and pleasure, for they have learnt the first rule of collecting: always buy the best example you can afford, whatever your field of interest and whatever the size of your purse. It is a simple rule, easy to practise and bound to bring pleasure and success.

You will find the rule easier to follow if you also make up your mind about damage and restoration. Inevitably many antiques have suffered over the years, and so restoration is a common problem. If you are concerned purely with investment you should try to avoid all damage, for the smallest imperfection or repair will affect the price of almost everything. However, most collectors need not be so strict. The pleasure to be drawn from antiques is rarely reduced by minor damage.

Restoration is sometimes necessary, but you should distinguish between restoration that merely puts back some of the quality already present in the object and restoration so total that it creates a new object. The latter type, to be found especially with furniture and ceramics, should be avoided for it aims frequently to deceive the buyer. On this level, the direct faker is more honest than the restorer. The ability to spot restoration can be greatly improved by some technical knowledge about how the object was made and the materials used. The collector should never scorn the chance to gain such knowledge.

These pocket pistols are hall-marked for 1823–4 and are typical of Joseph Egg's later weapons. Even by the firm's own high standards, the workmanship and attention to detail are remarkable.

Wonderful and exciting things have been produced by every age, but those of the last 150 years offer the greatest pleasure because they are accessible to collectors of even modest means.

Much has been written about the psychology of collecting, in order to explain its popularity. Such reasons as nostalgia, acquisitiveness, insecurity, competition and social unrest have been suggested. All such explanations have some basis in truth, but does it really matter why we collect? There is no need to analyse everything we do, for on this level analysis becomes a form of apology. Because we enjoy something, we feel compelled to explain it, justify it and apologize for it. Forget it. I have been a collector for years for three reasons: one, I had no choice for my parents were collectors and so some of my earliest memories revolve round antique shops; two, the pleasures of the chase and the pleasures of ownership; and three, I sometimes make some money out of it. The last is important only in that it allows my collection to grow and develop without costing too much.

LEFT A cross-shaped pendant of about 1780 made of diamonds and turquoises.

As my tastes change, so the old is used to finance the new.

It is a common mistake to put too much store on the investment potential of antiques. Most objects of quality will increase in value over a period of time, or they will at least keep pace with inflation. Sometimes the gain in value will be dramatic, sometimes the loss equally so. Art and antiques are a more precarious field for investment than the stock market because their popularity can so readily be influenced by fashion, and so those who regard them as an alternative are likely to have a difficult time. They may gain, but they will probably lose, and their concern for the simple value of the object will destroy all the pleasures of ownership. The only value of an antique is what someone is prepared to pay for it, and that is quite unpredictable. A share certificate on the other hand, while not an object of beauty, does follow a fairly predictable pattern of rise and fall in value. I am always rather pleased when individuals

or organizations come unstuck in their attempts to turn art and antiques into solid investment material for, by so doing, they have overlooked one basic fact: art and antiques exist primarily to give pleasure.

And this is why they were created in the first place, and why we continue to collect them. And this is why many books are produced about antiques, for they in their turn give pleasure by showing a wide range of popular antiques, to be enjoyed at secondhand. It is to be hoped that this book will give pleasure too.

9

Antiquities

Antiques are defined today as objects over one hundred years old, which is a relatively new classification. The year 1830 has been chosen as cut-off point because during the last three-quarters of the nineteenth century, makers of fine things largely followed a series of revivals of styles from earlier periods. For this reason it can be considered a less significant period in the history of antiques. It is, however, an extremely significant period in the history of antique-collecting, because it was precisely during this newly machine-dominated age, as copies proliferated, that originals became widely sought after and appreciated. Although great collections had been started among the very rich as early as the sixteenth century, it was not until the 'Grand Tour' drew the attention of travellers to the arts of other countries, that the less wealthy were prepared for the first time to pay more for the old than for the new. And as many of the richest families followed the twists and turns of fashion, replacing one style with another, their 'discards' became available for acquisition by those below them on the economic scale. In this way, the circle of people interested in antiques, for their diverse reasons, has become an ever-widening one.

By the same token, as original works became more valuable, copies were made more accurately and were passed off as originals. Faking became good business and was a major hazard to the collector. Every collector must always be on guard against fakes. They are obviously more common in more expensive pieces and here special care – and expert advice – should be taken. In furniture pieces are often 'made up', and it is important to know about the methods of old joiners and the sort of screws they used, and to be able to recognize genuine handles, hinges etc. Similar hazards await collectors of silver, porcelain, glass, and other objects. The only general advice can be: always examine an object with great care, and if there is something that seems out of place or out of character, beware; always take expert advice if you are making an expensive purchase.

Simple pottery objects are characteristic of a very early stage of human civilization, but techniques of shaping, painting and glazing can make it a very sophisticated art. Pottery, or earthenware, is made from clay, which varies in colour from white to reddish-brown, and in texture from coarse to very fine. The technique of throwing clay on a wheel was also known to many ancient

Greek vase, earthenware, amphora-shape, the black ground painted in red with Artemis watching a contest between Apollo and Heracles, about 500 BC.

peoples. The potter uses his hands to achieve the required shape as the wheel spins, or in the case of a tiny vessel, he can use a small tool. A lathe is then sometimes used for refinements.

Solid objects were made in clay moulds. Figures were made in sections and fused together with wet clay. Techniques of glazing were later discovered to seal the porous surface and enhance the beauty of pottery. Glazes may be of many colours, either opaque or translucent.

Perhaps the finest early pottery which can still be collected was made in Greece in the millennium before Christ. The earliest vessels had mainly geometric decoration, but around the sixth century BC potters began to paint designs of figures using the 'black-figure' technique and later the 'red-figure' technique. It is to the ornamental motifs and figured scenes of the Corinthian

and Athenian potters that we are indebted for much information about contemporary dress, furniture and social life.

Porcelain was first produced by the Chinese around AD 700, and they guarded the secret so well that they kept their monopoly until the early seventeenth century. When perfect, porcelain is hard, resonant to the strike, white and translucent when held against a strong light. It is achieved by mixing kaolin, a white china clay, with petuntze, a china stone of the generic group of rocks called felspar. A felspathic glaze used on hard-paste porcelain is made from the same material.

The early Chinese porcelain contained petuntze from different rock beds, which had an assortment of impurities, difficult to remove with primitive refinement techniques. This meant that the porcelain varied with the effect of the impurities it contained. Thus, unless the actual rock bed is known, it is difficult to imitate early specimens. When the mixture of kaolin and petuntze is fired at the correct temperature ($1,450°$C, $2,650°$F) in a kiln, true hard-paste porcelain results.

So-called soft-paste porcelain, which was first introduced into Europe at the end of the sixteenth century (hard-paste porcelain was finally discovered in the early eighteenth century), is not in fact a true porcelain, although it enabled European factories to imitate Chinese wares more successfully than with plain earthenware.

Gold and silver have always been symbolic of wealth, and sought after for the lustre they hold, their durability and their malleability. In fact they are too soft by themselves to attain proper toughness and so an alloy of other heavy metals, such as copper or platinum has to be used.

Gold is either mined or washed with water from auriferous gold-yielding deposits, or sluiced. A sluice is a long, sloping channel with constant running water, having a series of transverse bars to trap the gold, whose high density will cause it to sink. The Romans found that lining the trenches in the sluice with mercury resulted in a gold amalgam from which the mercury could subsequently be removed by heat. The cleaned gold ore must be powdered before the metal can be extracted by washing.

The colour of gold varies according to the quantity and type of alloy. Copper makes it redder, silver makes it greenish, and the addition of both copper and silver will pro-

duce a yellower tone than that of pure gold. White gold is three parts of gold mixed with one of platinum. The purity of gold today is measured in its carat value, that is the number of parts of pure gold in twenty-four; thus eighteen carat gold means eighteen parts of gold to six parts alloy, and the higher the carat the purer the gold.

Most silver is extracted from lead ore. The silver is purified from the ore by fractional melting, as lead has a much lower melting point. To purify gold and silver, temperatures of 1,065°C (1,950°F) and 1,000°C (1,830°F) respectively are needed. Wood fires can only achieve heats of around 700°C (1,290°F) which reddens but does not melt the metals. Therefore true metal working did not begin until higher temperatures became attainable with the use of artificial stimulation of the fire in the form of the furnace.

The discovery of glass-making is in the realm of legend. According to Pliny the secret was first discovered by chance when some sailors, who had made a fire on a sandy beach, noticed that by fusing sand (silica) with soda (alkali) and lime (calcium carbonate) a vitreous (glasslike) glaze resulted. They also found that if it was made thick enough it would not collapse, and it could be cut into small pieces for decoration, called mosaics. The paste could be pressed into open earthenware or metal moulds to make solid objects. Hollow vessels were made around sand cores, which were later removed. The oldest surviving glass objects are coloured beads made of pebbles coated with glass. These were exported all over the Mediterranean world from Egypt, Syria and Phoenicia from the fourth century BC.

The secret of glass blowing was discovered about 100 BC, probably also by chance, and this would have happened when a solid rod, used to hold the molten blob of glass, was replaced by a hollow tube. After that the amount of glass required was picked up red hot and quickly blown up to the right size. The vessel was shaped with accessory instruments, and handles and spouts sometimes added. From this period many objects survive, principally the ointment jars and larger vessels recovered undamaged from burial chambers, together with a number of pottery objects.

During the first four centuries AD two separate traditions emerged. The Syrians, who are credited with the discovery of glass blowing, made simple objects like flasks and

scent bottles, first in shades of green and yellow, and later in blues and purples. Decoration was naturalistic, and vases appear in the guise of shells or fruits, or moulded with human masks. Roman glassmakers, who also settled and worked in Alexandria, were more advanced, especially in their ability to control bright colours. They knew how to draw with an engraving tool and developed the arts of cutting the surface with grooves and facets from inside and out, and of carving in relief. A speciality was to carve and undercut at the same time so that the finished object looked as though it had a lacy coating attached by a series of tiny bridges. Another technique was that of laying opaque glass on a coloured base. It was then cut and ground away, leaving a cameo design in white against a deep coloured background. The finest example is the Portland vase, a black two-handled vessel decorated with white cameos.

Furnaces were simple to set up, and wherever the Roman armies conquered, glass-making spread, so that glass from the Roman period can be found throughout most of Europe and North Africa.

The earliest known furniture is that recovered from Egyptian tombs, followed by objects depicted on Greek pottery. The ancient Greeks were not wide-ranging in their forms. They concentrated on a few simple but elegant shapes, while perfecting the crafts of gilding, carving and joinery. Furniture was made from both native and imported timbers: maple, beech, cedar, oak and sycamore were among those available to them. Many of the thrones, couches and chests made by the Greeks show Egyptian influence. These items, together with chairs, tables and footstools appear to be all they considered necessary.

Typical features that recur on Egyptian, Greek and Roman furniture are animal forms for table supports and chair legs and backs, in particular swans, lions and winged sphinxes. Greek chairs, with their elegant sabre legs, have been prototypes for many succeeding generations, as have the couches and marble-topped tables found at Herculaneum and Pompeii.

With the disintegration of the Roman Empire around AD 500 classical culture as such was destroyed by the barbarian invaders, though many elements were preserved in the Byzantine Empire, founded in the fourth century, which grew and prospered throughout the medieval period. From the beginning its art was dedicated to the principle that the Emperor was God's representative on earth. Consequently the flavour of its culture is strongly religious. Lives of saints and biblical scenes are depicted on silver dishes, glass vessels, ivory carvings, mosaics, manuscripts, silk tapestries and metalwork of all kinds from many parts of the Byzantine Empire. Some lovely pieces of jewel-coloured glassware, now in St Mark's, Venice, were looted from Constantinople in the Fourth Crusade in 1204.

The major Islamic art forms with which we are concerned are pottery and glass. The Arabs, who by the eighth century ruled lands stretching from Spain to India, had very little culture of their own and were quick to absorb those of Egypt, Greece, Rome, Persia and Mesopotamia. In glass, the tradition of Alexandria was continued; thick, dark-coloured glass resembling precious stones was made and engraved with figurative decorations. The important centres were Rakka on the Euphrates, and Samarra and Baghdad on the Tigris. Decorations were similar to those on contemporary Persian and Egyptian ceramics.

Violet-coloured Aleppo glass came from Syria and was enhanced with floral patterns and geometrical designs, and glass made in Damascus was distinctly Chinese in feeling. It was in Damascus and Baghdad that the techniques of enamelling were brought to perfection. The finest mosque lamps were made in Persia and Syria; vase-shaped hanging vessels decorated with Arabic heraldry and inscriptions, from which they can often be dated.

The early Islamic pottery, while not so technically perfect as the cold hard enamels of contemporary Chinese porcelain, was warmer in feeling and more subdued. Shapes were simple, decoration harmonious. Floral and geometric motifs, spread over the whole surface, were the common form of decoration, since Islamic religion forbade the representation of living creatures.

The decorative arts of the European Middle Ages reflected the dominant styles of architecture. There were considerable commercial developments, and during the period 1100 to 1400, the first guilds of craftsmen were formed for protection against illegal and inferior competitors. Trading towns sprang up, and trade between nations increased in the way to which the East had long been accustomed. Leagues of trading cities were established, and with the rise of a merchant middle class, luxury goods were made for a larger public.

The earliest furniture of the Middle Ages was often plain and crude, though attempts to disguise the fact were made by painting it, and colourful hangings and carpets from the Middle East and fine textiles from Italy were draped on walls and tables to soften the effect. The main item to be found in every large house was the marriage chest. French ones were sometimes covered with iron scrollwork; the English decorated theirs with arched panelling and Gothic motifs derived from church architecture, as did the Dutch and Germans. Italian *cassoni* carved and painted were the finest of all.

In northern Europe, most furniture was made from oak, but chestnut, walnut and cypress were more plentiful in Italy, southern France and Spain. Pine furniture naturally predominated in Alpine regions.

Very little fine pottery was produced in Europe in the Middle Ages outside Spain. The Arabs imposed Islamic traditions and introduced the arts of tin-glazed (a white pottery glaze) and lustred earthenware. The latter were vases and dishes glazed

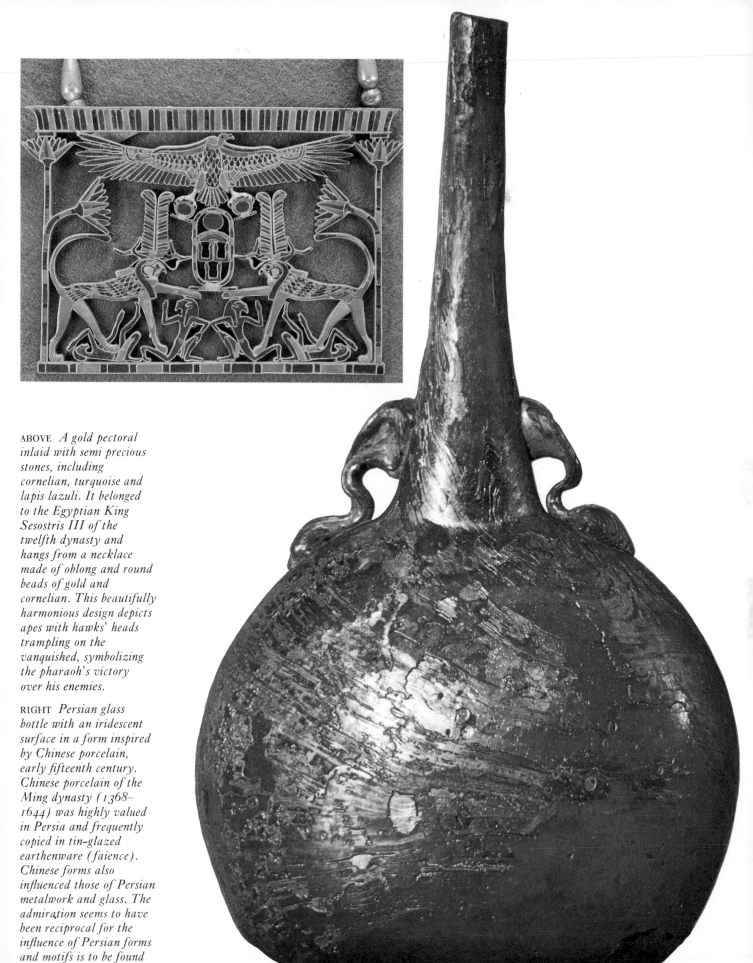

ABOVE *A gold pectoral inlaid with semi precious stones, including cornelian, turquoise and lapis lazuli. It belonged to the Egyptian King Sesostris III of the twelfth dynasty and hangs from a necklace made of oblong and round beads of gold and cornelian. This beautifully harmonious design depicts apes with hawks' heads trampling on the vanquished, symbolizing the pharaoh's victory over his enemies.*

RIGHT *Persian glass bottle with an iridescent surface in a form inspired by Chinese porcelain, early fifteenth century. Chinese porcelain of the Ming dynasty (1368–1644) was highly valued in Persia and frequently copied in tin-glazed earthenware (faience). Chinese forms also influenced those of Persian metalwork and glass. The admiration seems to have been reciprocal for the influence of Persian forms and motifs is to be found in Chinese porcelain.*

17

Stirrup pots, so called because of the shape of the spouts, are characteristic of the pottery found in Ecuador, Peru, and Columbia, and rarely in North America. They have little practical use, and were ceremonial or funerary vessels, sometimes filled with wine; some of them emit a low whistling sound when liquid is poured from them. These are of the Mochican people, who lived along the west coast of Peru, and date from around AD 600.

with the metallic lustre of copper or silver. These wares are usually known as Hispano-Moresque. A speciality was to paint the arms of a family in a circle of foliage or petals. After this idea caught on among Italian noblemen Italian craftsmen began to make their own imitations, and they were followed by other Europeans.

The gradual decline of Islamic glass coincided with the establishment of the Venetian glassworks in 1291 on the island of Murano. During the fourteenth century the glass industry of Murano continued to produce coloured wares, and started to make glass mirrors, replacing those of polished metal. Rather poor quality bubble-ridden glassware for the table was also made, but it was not until the sixteenth century that something approaching clear crystal glass was achieved.

By 1400 the techniques of working precious metals were well advanced. As with furniture, the style in Germany, northern Europe and England reflected contemporary Gothic architecture. Decoration frequently included precious stones, Gothic lettering and entire enamelled figurines of

ABOVE *A rare example of a Byzantine drinking vessel said to have been in the possession of Lorenzo de' Medici. The bowl is of mottled sardonyx in varying shades of brown and white, hollowed out and ribbed on the outside. The gold lining is folded over to form an outer lip, which is tooled with two rows of beading, enclosing a band of stars and trimmed with pierced petal shapes.*

LEFT *A gold mask pendant from Peru. The exact purpose of this pendant mask is open to speculation. Several gold funerary masks have been discovered but their symbolic significance is unknown.*

19

saints. Tracery is reminiscent of that on thrones and pulpits, while designs of foot supports and finials of vessels were copied from the crockets and pinnacles of contemporary stonework.

Fine quality tooling occurred on flat metalwork (plate) provided it was thin enough. Five terms are often used loosely, and need clarification: punching refers to indentations on the surface made by a plain or shaped punch; embossing means decoration raised up in relief on the upper surface from the back; chasing is in effect embossing from the front. When elaborate scenes and patterns, contained both embossed and chased relief, this is referred to as repoussé. The process called gilding is the application of gold on to the surface of baser metals including silver. It was known in ancient times, and by the Middle Ages was in such common use that it encouraged fraudulent practices: any metal could be passed off as gold. Gold and silver alloys could also contain more base metals than necessary without it being apparent. Thus the first guilds were largely occupied with devising tests and enforcing regulations whereby a standard could be guaranteed. The only controls stringent enough were those established by the English.

The first flowering of the Renaissance was in the Italian city states, which were well provided with wealthy banking families inclined to patronize the arts. The rediscovery of ancient civilizations led to a new affinity with Classical antiquity. A style based on the purer forms of Greece and Rome emerged, and Italian craftsmen were lured to the important European centres to diffuse their ideas and their skills.

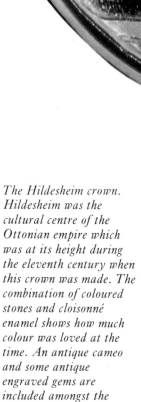

The Hildesheim crown. Hildesheim was the cultural centre of the Ottonian empire which was at its height during the eleventh century when this crown was made. The combination of coloured stones and cloisonné enamel shows how much colour was loved at the time. An antique cameo and some antique engraved gems are included amongst the stones.

Furniture, even in the great palaces, was still sparse, and depended on lavish use of upholstery and hangings for colour and richness. Cupboards and chests were made to look like monuments with columnar supports. Cassoni took on a sarcophagus-like appearance of Egyptian derivation. With the addition of wings and backs to simple seats, the first sofas were created. Greater use of figurative carving was made and the first bronze handles appeared on cupboards. Painted scenes were still a form of decoration; gradually the triumphs of Roman generals gained favour over religious scenes as subject matter. Wood was both polished and gilded (gold on wood) and magnificent marble-topped tables mounted on richly carved supports were made for the great houses. Decorative motifs included sphinxes, nymphs and masks amid elaborate arrangements of foliage, together with human and mythical figures. As the style gradually spread northwards, each country developed its own interpretations.

Renaissance silver and silver gilt lost the Gothic formality of the preceding centuries, and new, intricate designs of strapwork and repoussé were used. The ideas of the great Italian silversmith Benvenuto Cellini (1500–69) spread to France and then England; and to the few pieces of domestic plate that were already in general use (salts, ewers and basins, and tall drinking cups) were added beakers and tankards, spoons, and flatware. Two-handled cups appeared, the handles often in the form of elongated human torsos, with decorations derived from Roman murals.

An example of Roman cameo carving in onyx. This fourth-century AD cameo depicts the capture of the Emperor Valerian by Shapur I of Persia in AD 260. The drama and movement of the scene has been skilfully depicted by the cameo cutter on a tiny scale.

21

Maps and Prints

Maps By definition a map is a graphic statement of direction and contour. It endeavours to represent three-dimensional surfaces on two-dimensional paper in such a way that a real appreciation of the terrain is conveyed to the reader of the map.

Modern cartographers have provided accurate maps of the world, moon and other celestial bodies, but to do this they all used advanced scientific techniques including aerial surveys. The early mapmakers, although endeavouring to make their work as accurate as possible, were limited to crude and inadequate equipment. During the fifteenth century when the earliest maps were produced, there was little background knowledge and few reference sources available to the cartographer; in fact, during this period it was not possible to establish longitude with any real accuracy, neither was there an established unit of measurement. In England the mile of 1,760 yards (1,610 m) became statutory for London and Westminster in 1593, and with the expansion of the postal services in the seventeenth century it became the accepted unit for the post-mile throughout the kingdom.

Fifteenth-century cartographers did not avail themselves of all the then known print-ing techniques, some of which involved the refinement of tonal graduations, but confined themselves to relief and intaglio blocks. Lithography made its debut during the nineteenth century, and whilst a number of collectors will consider this period too late for serious study, many interesting and attractive maps made their appearance.

The relief process was used mainly on woodblocks. The map design was drawn (in reverse) on the woodblock with ink, and with the aid of a knife, or graver, the engraver proceeded to cut away all the wood not marked in ink to a depth of about one-sixteenth of an inch (1.5 mm) or more, leaving the inked design standing proudly in relief.

The woods used generally for the blocks were pear, apple, lime and other soft woods; later boxwood in thicker sections superseded the softer types.

The intaglio process is the opposite of relief. The block in this process consisted of a sheet of copper, flat and thick enough to be rigid when taking impressions. The design was traced first on the copper; then, with a burin or graver, it was cut into the copper. By varying the pressure on the cutting tool the engraver was able to cut a groove of varying depth in the metal, which

SUSSEX

PART PART OF OF

SURREY

KENT

The Scale of Miles

THE BRITISH SEA

4

A MAP OF
VIRGINIA
AND
MARYLAND

Sold by Thomas Bassit in Fleetstreet
and Richard Chiswell in St Pauls
Church yard

A Scale of English Miles

VIRGINIA

MARYLAND

CAROLINA

PART OF

CHESEAPEAKE BAY

Minquaas

Safsquahana

Konekotays

Tockwoghs

Minquaas

Sauwan

THE NORTH SEA.

PART OF
NEW IARSY.

DÉP.^t DU FINISTÈRE.

A COMPARATIVE VIEW OF
THE PRINCIPAL
WATERFALLS, ISLANDS, LAKES, RIVERS
AND
MOUNTAINS,
IN
THE WESTERN HEMISPHERE.

Sporting engraving entitled Partridge-Hawking, *published in 1710 by Richard Blome in his* Gentleman's Recreation, *a survey of field sports and other activities.*

familiar with metal-working through the manufacture of mathematical instruments, turned to the intaglio or line-engraving process for the maps.

Decoration on early fifteenth-century maps was more or less restricted to the borders. The first half of the sixteenth century saw the ornamental cartouches, usually imitative of wood-carved scrolls, and the compass indicator, dividers, coats-of-arms, ships, cherubs, figures, and a host of other decorative devices.

The period from the mid-sixteenth century to the eighteenth is undoubtedly the one that interests collectors most. It was a period during which decorative cartography and technical achievement combined to produce maps of the finest quality.

Maps have been hand-coloured, to enhance them artistically and to embolden their engraved symbols, since the earliest days of their history.

In the Netherlands artists already skilled in the art of illumination turned their attention to the colouring of maps, and by the middle of the sixteenth century map colouring had become a recognized trade. Map colourists worked either as independents, or as employees of map engravers. Not all maps were coloured; it was possible to purchase either 'coloured' or 'plain'. Today, maps with early or original colouring are generally more appreciated, and in consequence command higher prices.

Maps were, of course, printed in black on white paper and, to avoid continual reference for the heraldic colours, some engravers indicated the required tint by engraving small alphabetical letters in the spaces and quarters.

Other engravers used a method of shading and stippling to indicate the colours. A close look at a John Speed map, for instance, will reveal small alphabetical letters representing the initials of the colours, or tinctures.

Unfortunately there are many maps engraved with heraldic symbols and coats-of-arms that do not have these colours indicated by either method, which means that modern colourists of old uncoloured maps have to research the information, and if this becomes too tedious, there is a risk of colours being added for effect, rather than for accuracy.

Ptolemy's *Geographia*, produced in Alexandria about AD 160, referred to methods of mapmaking, but it was not until the fif-

produced either a coarse or fine line on the finished impression.

From the mid-sixteenth century until 1820 copper was almost invariably the metal used, although very occasionally brass, zinc, iron and even silver were used. From 1820 steel, being a harder metal and in consequence more durable, slowly gained popularity over copper.

In the early fifteenth century and up to the middle of the sixteenth, the woodblock was the favoured means of producing maps. By the mid-sixteenth century the cartographers of the Netherlands, already teenth century that mapmaking as such developed, and although primarily concerned with assisting the traveller and recording land parcels, it must be assumed that, even in the fifteenth century, maps were appreciated as works of art just as much as for any scientific merit.

Early cartographers, like any other section of the community, had to earn a living, either by direct selling, as an employee, or by being patronized. Therefore, market requirements must have influenced the finished product, especially during a period when there was a natural tendency to combine the functional with the artistic.

Although antique maps cover the entire surface of the world, they were nearly all of European origin. The Dutch, Italian, German, French and English were the predominant mapmakers from the fifteenth to the eighteenth century.

A point worth noting in respect of dates

Woodcut by Albrecht Dürer, St Joachim and St Anne at the Golden Gate, *published in 1509.*

27

shown on maps: these usually refer to the *original* issue, but as maps were often printed for years after without any alterations being made to the plate, the actual date of issue of a particular map can be much later than the date indicated on it. This last point also applies to many prints.

Prints The earliest method of print-making was by means of wood-cutting and wood-engraving. On a woodcut the drawing stands out in relief and when inked leaves a black impression, whereas a wood-engraving is carved out leaving the surround in relief to be inked so that a white impression on a black background is obtained. It can readily be seen that both wood-cutting and wood-engraving can be used on the same block – and frequently are, to give the most astonishing effects of light and shade or *chiaroscuro*.

In the hands of such a master as Albrecht Dürer wood-cutting became a major means of artistic expression, and it particularly lent itself to the expression of the rather morbid, fantastical work produced by the German artists of the period.

Line-engraving was the principal process used by artists in the seventeenth and eighteenth centuries. The drawing is cut in lines with a needle-sharp scoop called a burin on a smooth copper plate, and is then inked so that when paper is pressed on to the plate the impression of the design is transferred to the paper. Many impressions can be taken from the same plate, but since most metal plates tend to wear with use, imperfections creep into the later prints. Consequently most print makers limited, and indeed still limit, even with the refinements of contemporary metal manufacture and printing methods, the edition of any single engraving to a comparatively small number. Variation in texture and shading is achieved by the use of different instruments to cut into the metal.

Hogarth was one of many artists in the eighteenth century who was well known as an engraver before he made his name as a painter. His famous series on the evils of London was immensely popular and prints of the Harlots' Progress are said to have sold 1,000 copies in the first edition.

Another form of plate engraving, which was used to perfection by Rembrandt, is the etching. The whole plate is covered with some substance impervious to acid and the drawing is made in it. The plate is then submerged in acid which eats into the metal where the substance has been removed, and by recovering the drawing and submerging it several times the artist has far greater means of variation of tone than he has had before. When the process is finished the plate is inked and printed in just the same manner as a burin engraving.

The most famous of old master etchers is Rembrandt. Rembrandt's etching of *Christ with the Sick*, printed in 1649, soon became known as the *Hundred-Guilder Print*, for even in Rembrandt's own lifetime it cost that sum of money to buy a

ABOVE *Etching by Rembrandt*, The Goldweigher's Field, *published in 1651.*

RIGHT *Engraving by William Hogarth (1697-1764) from the series entitled* The Rake's Progress, *published in 1735.*

copy. He used the medium in the most exciting manner to represent effects of light and shade, and some of his finest etchings are of night scenes or of places in near-darkness, notably *The Adoration of the Shepherds* of 1652.

Another variant on the theme of engraving, and one which we shall find to be of particular importance in the development of the late eighteenth and early nineteenth century print, is the *mezzotint*. In this process, the engraver works on the plate with rocker and scraper. The rocker stipples the surface of the plate in dots, instead of lines, and the remainder of the unrocked surface is then worked on with scraper and burin. The plate is printed as for an ordinary engraving – with this extremely important difference, that the crests made by the stippling pierce the surface of the paper in the printing causing,

according to Davenport's memorable phrase 'a certain disintegration of the substance into something distinctly resembling the pile of velvet'.

Rembrandt also pioneered the use of landscape as a subject for printmakers, a subject that became increasingly popular in the eighteenth century. As travel became more fashionable throughout Europe, many artists of the calibre of Canaletto began to produce a great variety of topographical and landscape etchings and engravings. The popularity of this type of print continued through the nineteenth century, when topographical prints became the forerunners of modern souvenirs.

That printmaking closely reflected social patterns of behaviour and fashion is also borne out by the sporting print, an equally popular genre of the eighteenth and early nineteenth centuries. Interest in land-

scape included the related rural pursuits, of which hunting is the most obvious example.

One more printing method remains to be mentioned – lithography. This is a process originally perfected by Alois Senefelder in 1793, and consists of drawing the design upon a stone in greasy crayon or oil-based ink. Water is poured over it and then an oil-based ink which only clings to the greasy drawing; paper is then pressed upon the stone, and a print results. In these days the lithographic stone has been replaced by a zinc plate which for most practical purposes is as effective, and much easier to handle than the bulky heavy stones of former times.

All the printing about which we have spoken so far was in black or one-coloured ink on white paper; but early on in the history of print-making, master craftsmen began to experiment with colour. The first English colour-printer recorded was Elisha Kirkhall. In 1724 he printed a two-coloured seascape from a single plate; and four years later made fifty full colour plates after van Huysum to illustrate a book on flowers, John Martyn's *Historia Plantarum Rariorum*, in which he combined etching and

mezzotinting in several colours which were then retouched by hand.

All these processes were developed in the nineteenth century. George Baxter combined mezzotint plates with woodblock printing in oiled inks, and made reproductions of any picture so cheaply that he was able to advertise that 'while their artistic beauty may procure for them a place in the Royal palaces throughout Europe the prices at which they are retailed introduces them to the humblest cottages.'

Many of these new processes were exploited during the latter part of the nineteenth century by artists, and printmaking once again became a valid part of the repertoire of painters and sculptors. Chromolithography enabled painters such as Lautrec and Mucha to revolutionize the poster; similar work was produced in America by Will Bradley. At the same time the older processes enjoyed a new vogue; in the work of the American painter James McNeill Whistler, the etching reached a level of artistic quality equivalent to that it had attained in the seventeenth century.

In the United States of America the history of print-making only really begins

Etching by Antonio Canaletto (1697–1768), from a series of 34 views of Venice and its surrounding countryside first published in 1744. Some of the views are imaginary, while others, like this one, The Lock at Dolo, *were based on actual scenes.*

AMERICAN EXPRESS TRAIN.

after the War of Independence – before that most of what little print work there was had been brought over from Europe. There were, of course, exceptions to this general rule. The celebrated Paul Revere made a hand-coloured engraving of *The Boston Massacre* of 1770; and a little later, at the time of the Declaration of Independence, Edward Savage made a series of engraved and mezzotint portraits of famous people including Washington, Franklin and Adams. Another painter, Rembrandt Peale was awarded the silver medal of the Franklin Institution in 1827 for his lithographed copy of his own oil portrait of George Washington.

As in Europe, lithographic printers opened up print workshops which produced large editions of prints for the general public. One of the most successful of these in the early days was Anthony Imbert, whose printing workshop opened in New York in 1825. Among his subsequent publications were a series of New York scenes by the architect A. J. Davis and the series of Red Indian drawings by the famous Catlin.

Probably the best known print publishers in the States were Currier and Ives (Currier alone from 1836 to 1857; and Ives thereafter until 1901). They made many hundreds of series of popular prints – of the occurrences of the time, sporting prints, portraits and landscapes. Some of their most pleasant were the New York landscapes by Frances Farmer.

With the transatlantic arrival of techniques similar to Baxter's, full chromolithography hit America with force. The first recorded series was printed by Max Rosenthal who set up his press in Philadelphia in 1849, and had the title *Wild Scenes and Wild Hunters*. Thereafter, as in Europe and especially in England, printmaking was as bad or as good as the artists who made the master drawings and the workmen who did the printing. The best artists naturally supervised their own prints, one of the most notable series being those by the painter Winslow Homer entitled *Campaign Sketches of the Civil War* printed and published by Perry of Boston, Massachusetts. Coloured lithographs were used for theatre bills, book illustrations and music covers; and line engravings were the normal method of newspaper illustration, from which grew the American, and later world-wide, passions for comics.

An American train of the Hudson River Railroad, an example of the lithographs produced by Currier & Ives that did much to popularize the American landscape and its society.

31

The collector of prints has two immense advantages over his fellows in other fields of collecting – range of places where he may hope to discover additions to his collection, and range of prices. Yet another recommendation is that a collection of prints can be built up to complement another interest, be it botany, architecture or whatever. Because the print was the pre-camera version of, for example, the book illustration, the pin-up and the newspaper cartoon, and because it was natural for the eighteenth-century bookseller to open up a print department for engravings, etchings and mezzotints, and later for chromolithographs and similar confections, one still finds many second-hand and antiquarian bookshops with a stock of prints of considerable interest.

Then again, virtually every illustrated book before 1900 has prints of one kind or another as illustrations, in addition to the massive number of books *of* prints with commentary – for example those by Ackermann and Finden. Many of these books have now been taken to pieces and the prints sold individually; but it is always as well for a collector, should he buy such a volume cheaply, to collate it on the off-chance that it is complete, for the complete volume is infinitely more valuable and desirable than the sum of its individual prints.

RIGHT *Poster printed by lithography, designed by Will Bradley. The Chap Book was an American magazine rather similar to the English Yellow Book. Bradley worked in a style close to that of the better known English designer, Aubrey Beardsley.*

BELOW *Poster printed by lithography designed by the French artist Toulouse-Lautrec. The bold colours and the free design show the influence of Japanese prints. In the hands of the leading artists of the time, such as Lautrec, the poster came of age in France at the end of the nineteenth century.*

Silver and Gold

At the beginning of the twentieth century any silver lacking the pedigree of good English hallmarks would be found lurking at the back of American closets, for the true merit of Colonial silver was still unrecognized in the States and unseen by the rest of the world. It was not that these marks had much meaning; it was more that they proclaimed the plate to be English, or Scottish, or Irish, and therefore desirable. Few marks had been deciphered at the time, for the English hallmarking system was never intended as a code to be read by all, but as an aid to the maintenance of law within the goldsmith's craft. This has proved to be of advantage to the English, for the story those marks are able to tell increases interest in the silver itself.

The earliest American craftsmen were London trained, but as they had crossed the Atlantic to escape English restrictions, they desired no guilds for the protection of their work such as they had in England. In London the Worshipful Company of Goldsmiths, who had been given a Royal Charter in 1327, stamped the mark of the leopard's head on silver they had tested and proved to be of sterling standard, so that they could punish the maker (known after 1363 by his own mark, stamped alongside the leopard's head) if his work was unsatisfactory. In Boston, Robert Sanderson (1608–93) gladly punched his personal mark but it was the boast of American goldsmiths that they needed no supervision and even the word *sterling* was not stamped on their silver until after 1850, when it had largely ceased to be hand-made anyway.

The sterling standard, 92.5 per cent pure silver to 7.5 per cent copper, was first perfected in Germany many centuries before being adopted in England, where no lesser standard was ever used legally. The finest Continental silver was also of this standard, but as each silver-making centre was independently ruled, no standards were invariable in any given country. English silver coins had also been of the sterling standard and it was probably because this was debased that Goldsmith's Hall introduced the mark of the *lion passant* in 1544, to show invariable quality. With the date letter, which appeared officially in 1478, this made a total of four marks on London Plate and, like the maker's mark, was probably copied from Montpelier in France, who had already used it.

More than 150 silversmiths were recorded in Boston alone before 1800. Sanderson, his partner John Hull (1624–83) and other

RIGHT *The nautilus cup is typical of the elaborate drinking vessels produced by silversmiths in Nuremberg and Augsburg between 1550 and 1650, and is clearly influenced by High Renaissance and Mannerist designs from Italy. The shell was cleaned and ground down until the iridescent mother-of-pearl showed through. The cup was made by Nikolaus Schmidt of Nuremberg in about 1590, and forms part of the table silver at Buckingham Palace.*

FAR RIGHT *It is thought that this elaborate gold and jasper salt was made for Louis XI of France about 1460. Typically Gothic in style, its eight arches support the upper base, decorated with filigree work.*

immigrants, fired by enthusiasm for the new, free life, made high quality silver and trained others to keep up these standards. The goldsmiths of New York set up their workshops about a generation later, men with Dutch names who made silver in the Dutch style, although under English rule, while the first of Philadelphia's craftsmen appeared in the 1690s, making silver for wealthy Quakers who required quality without frills. Canada's first goldsmiths also started work in the late seventeenth century, almost entirely in Quebec and Montreal. They worked largely for the Church and the designs were very French in concept.

The American porringer was the first distinctively trans-Atlantic item of silver to be made that had no real English equivalent. These medium-sized, flat, shallow bowls, with a single pierced handle, were found in quantity in almost every New England home and were entirely domestic in use. Piercing on the handles, which also had initials engraved, were at first a subject of much variety, although later it became almost universally keyhole. In New York, where fewer porringers were made, piercing was often so intricate that no space remained for initials, a loss to the silver historian, for tracing the family tree connected with initials in America replaced the interest hallmarks bestowed in England.

In the last half of the seventeenth century

the English made two-handled cups of German derivation, also known as porringers or sometimes caudle cups, the name given to the simplified form made in America. There they were never larger than one person could hold comfortably, but in England these richly embossed bowls varied in size from being quite small to being large enough to hold a gallon or more.

These cups draw attention to another, extraordinarily atttactive, New York two-handled bowl, made in the seventeenth and eighteenth centuries. It was developed from the Dutch brandy bowl used for holding raisins soaked in brandy which were eaten straight from the bowl with silver spoons on special family occasions. In New York they were oval, as in Holland after 1670, and shallow in proportion to width, and often commemorated a marriage. They were incised with deep lines, forming six sections, in which curved panels enclosed embossed, or engraved floral decoration.

Candles must have been as important to

RIGHT *Gold cups were made throughout Europe in the early seventeenth century. This one was produced in Salzburg. Its bowl curves up into a flared lip, and the scrolling handles take the form of elongated female figures. The cup stands on a knopped and stepped trumpet stem, the whole decorated in enamel with emblems and heraldry in the Renaissance style.*

BELOW *This silver teapot comes from a five-piece service made by the American silversmith Samuel Kirk in 1828. He worked in Baltimore, where, in an attempt to emulate the British hallmarking system, silversmiths were compelled to mark their wares with their initials or marks, as well as date letters. During the post-Federal period there was a vogue for all-over embossing and for rectangular handles.*

life in America as elsewhere, but very few holders survive in silver, one exception being a pair in the French clustered-column style, engraved 1686, by Jeremiah Dummer (1645–1718), the first American-born silversmith in Boston. Holders were also comparatively rare in England before 1700, when they were gloriously simple, but examples after that date are collectors' favourites, and have remained popular and expensive, particularly those made all through the eighteenth century by the great Huguenot craftsmen.

It was not until the city of Sheffield started specializing in holders in 1773 that they became easier on the purse. They are stamped on the base with hallmarks that include the extra punch of a crown, denoting silver made in Sheffield, and after 1784 the sovereign's head was stamped on all English silver to show a duty paid. The smiths of an industrial city like Sheffield were determined to cut costs by mechanizing the craft, while still producing the latest styles. They used such thin machine-rolled silver that the sticks required leading to hold their shape. These methods continued to evolve so that Sheffield-made candlesticks are always cheaper than those of London, but are also renowned for variety and quality of design.

Church plate was made in Britain and America, but at the time that the old Mass chalices were replaced by new communion cups in England, mostly between about 1565 and 1580, the ancestors of those who founded the New World were kneeling in the churches of English villages and towns. Many of those lovely cups survive, but the colonists who went to Massachusetts had more in common with the Scottish kirk, which allowed vessels to be used in the home and taken to church on Sundays. Of these the beaker, used all over the north of Scotland, was the most popular in Boston.

Both in shape and decoration this beaker is very like the Dutch beakers so popular in the Scottish kirk, which were taken to Aberdeen originally by students from Leyden University in Holland. They were copied by the Scots profusely and later simplified, but were always more interesting than those made in London or Norwich, which also had close connections with the Dutch. The form in New England soon changed, becoming very varied, but more than a century later the link with Aberdeen was further strengthened when the first

bishop of America was consecrated there in 1784, London having refused to help out a rebel.

The tankard was another secular drinking vessel taken to church in America, a use that could never have been contemplated in England where it was too well imbued with the convivial spirit. Often very large, holding several pints, it was originally used for communal drinking, which sometimes led to fighting. The Scandinavians had the answer to this with their peg tankard

designed to keep any one man from taking more than his share by the insertion of a measured row of pegs down the inside. From about 1650 these were squat and drum-shaped, raised on three feet of the ball and claw design, or in the shape of a pomegranate, or even a lion, with the thumbpiece frequently matching. Sometimes they had a coin inserted in the lid.

The everyday English tankard at the time was still inclined to be large and, until about 1700, drum-shaped, a little taller in proportion to width than the very squat Scandinavian type, with a flat stepped lid, a beautifully engraved coat of arms on the body and a fine thumbpiece. One of the most effective of these is a *lion couchant*, sprawling lazily across and on to the lid, and very occasionally the bowl is also supported on three lion feet.

The American tankard was small by comparison, rarely holding more than a pint, and was often soberly inscribed on the handle with the initials of both husband and wife. In basic shape it evolved less than in England, where date can be told at a glance by lid and body features, and it continued with the flat top much longer. The domed lid, which in England was normal from about 1710 onwards, appeared more

consistently in Philadelphia, but when used in Boston it was also surmounted by a moulded finial for a while. Paul Revere (1735–1818) made several of these in his early period, with an interesting cast finial, the round body broken by a raised rib, as in England. Arms were also engraved on the tankards quite frequently, in both Boston and Philadelphia.

Despite these English points the American tankard was altogether distinctive, one positive feature being the shield at the tip of the handle, in varying shapes, usually bearing an applied mask that was totally individual. In addition there was a beaded drop, or a rat-tail down the handle from the hinge, which might also have cut card or other decoration on it. The thumbpiece was usually scroll, or corkscrew in New York, only occasionally becoming more ambitious.

It is said that the collector's period in England started in 1660 when the Civil War was over and demands that plate be converted to coin gave way to an exuberance of richly decorated silver, Dutch and German in concept, in a gay and carefree age. However in 1697 the Britannia standard was introduced, raising the proportion of silver in the alloy used above that of sterling,

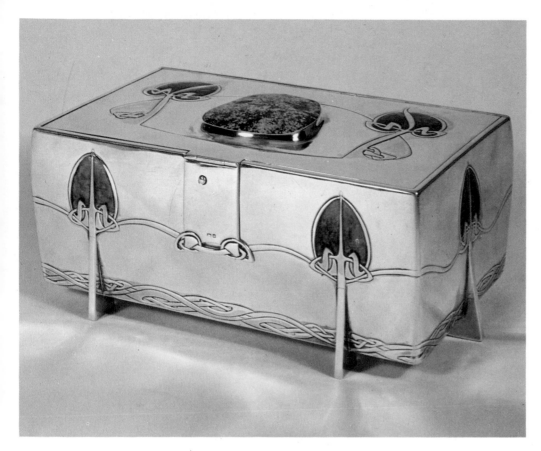

A superb Liberty 'Cymric' enamelled silver box inset with a turquoise matrix. Designed by Archibald Knox, this piece is one of a very small group of such boxes, and is one of the finest examples of English Art Nouveau silver.

making the metal too soft for such decoration. A period of superlative work in heavy gauge silver followed, which was domestic in character with lovely lines and a rich, glowing patina. The designs were influenced overwhelmingly by the first Huguenots to arrive from France, the forerunners of men like Paul de Lamerie who took the craft through the Rococo period and were working at its height (1705–51). The sterling standard returned at the option of the maker in 1719 but for the majority the collector's period could not really be said to start until mechanized mills produced thin rolled silver in about 1770, and the Neo-Classic period began.

In America the war that cooled the melting pots did not take place before 1775, and even then their own Civil War (1861–5) was to come, with a demand on silver plate that amounted to extinction in the south, where goldsmiths had been strongly active. Nevertheless good domestic silver was made in all the American centres throughout the eighteenth century, largely to private order, as it always had been, because silver itself was scarce and used largely for important family occasions, permanently recorded by the engraving of initials and inscriptions. Styles became increasingly English, concentrating more upon workmanship and line than the latest fashion, spurning decoration beyond the use of gadroons or cut card applications in limited amounts, with armorials engraved on plain surfaces. After independence was gained in 1781 such anglicisms were frowned on, but the empty space looked so bare that initials were often dressed up to give the same impression.

The Greek revival was delayed in America by the Revolution, but was then equally popular. Any form of domestic hollow-ware, whether cylindrical or urn-shaped, was suitable for light, symmetrical decoration, piercing or bright cut engraving, and Boston teapots sometimes also had fluted drums, to lovely effect, particularly in the hands of Paul Revere. In Philadelphia beading was very frequently used around the edges as the only decoration, a form known on similar pots by Hester Bateman (1774–89) of London, but the pierced gallery surrounding the top of objects such as coffee pots or urn-shaped sugar bowls, often in addition to beading, was unmistakably Philadelphian in an age when silver was becoming more collectable.

For those with a taste for the antique but little space, bucket forks are among the

oldest examples of American silver, while miniature caudle cups, just over an inch high, were also very early. Spoons provide the greatest variety, since in England before 1700 a plethora of provincial marks, themselves a collector's subject, can be found on spoons with finely sculptured finials. The Apostle spoon is a well-known design, with figures on the end of the usual hexagonal stem and fig-shaped bowl. In America, the New York hoof or caryatid terminal is rare, but there is an enormous range of trifids, coffin end, fiddle and other patterns and in particular of the picture backs.

The tiny caddy spoons in England cast in endless different shapes, some purely ornamental, are also very popular with collectors. They were well made, particularly in Birmingham, which has the anchor as its town mark.

Sugar tongs of the scissor type, with shell grips, were made in America from about 1750, in England somewhat earlier. Their stems were never alike, while later pincher tongs are enormously varied in decoration, and are often bright cut, embossed or pierced and are among the least expensive to buy though rewarding to collect.

Ingenious and quite delightful are the baby corals and rattles that were made by all nations from the time of the ancient Egyptians to the nineteenth century. Most of them are beautifully engraved, as are the rows of silver bells, and teething whistles. Patch boxes too, were made in most countries, for all ladies like to beautify themselves, and keep their adornments in nicely decorated silver boxes with a detachable lid. Round or oval tobacco boxes were rather larger than patch boxes but had similar lids. Snuff boxes on the other hand had hinged lids since gentlemen took snuff at any time, perhaps on horseback when they would not have both hands free. These were made superlatively in Birmingham as were nutmeg graters, carried individually for the seasoning of food; vinaigrettes, for personal freshness; wine labels and other small objects, all good subjects for collection. Vinaigrettes were especially attractive with their beautifully pierced grilles inside tiny boxes, and were made to look like anything that took the craftsman's fancy, such as a fish, animal, strawberry, or flower.

The finest snuff boxes are French, gold and richly jewelled; nevertheless, those

41

George III six-piece tea and coffee set, by R. & D. Hennell, 1797. In the most pleasing Neo-Classic lines, this set is obviously handmade.

made in Birmingham by Nathaniel Mills in the early nineteenth century are first class, with their repoussé tops, mostly depicting castles, cathedrals and other topographical subjects, and their strongly cast sides or borders. Other makers created boxes with pastoral, sporting, mythological or commemorative scenes, and although snuff boxes were also made in London and elsewhere, on the whole they are less imaginative. The great names of Birmingham displayed the same characteristics in their caddy spoons, vinaigrettes, wine labels and other small things, and between them did more for the small collector than any other group of men.

While the styles of Neo-Classicism, the Renaissance and the Gothic revival dominated the first half of the nineteenth century, the most important stylistic development of the second half of the nineteenth century was the assimilation of Japanese designs and methods into period furniture and metalwork by English, American and French craftsmen.

Tiffany and Company and another great American commercial firm, the Gorham Company of New York, produced many 'Japanese' pieces, especially Gorham's beautiful copper examples, characterized by the use of contrastingly applied metals.

Japanese metalworkers, engaged in making highly ornate sword furniture, perfected this technique. After the wearing of swords was banned in Japan in 1876, American and English silversmiths provided employment for many Japanese metalworkers. The use of Japanese motifs – flowering plants, bamboo, birds, insects – was extremely popular, and much American silver is bright cut with such patterns.

The Art Nouveau movement in England, between roughly 1885 and 1910, grew out of the theories of designers such as Morris, who emphasized the importance of the individual craftsman and designer. In a sense, of course, the great strength of the arts and crafts ideal was also its weakness; mass industrialization was an inexorable development which could not be stemmed least of all by the attempts of a few high-minded individuals.

The Art Nouveau period nevertheless produced many fine designers. The most important are Charles Robert Ashbee, who started the school and Guild of Handicrafts, Gilbert Marks, Nelson and Edith Dawson, Omar Ramsden and his partner Alwyn Carr.

The English firm, Liberty's, produced much Art Nouveau silver. Although the designers were cloaked in anonymity, three have been identified: Archibald Knox, Rex Silver and Bernard Cuzner. The finest Liberty silver was produced under the brand name 'Cymric'; while a range of high quality pewter, was marketed under the name 'Tudric'.

Short Glossary of Terms

Acanthus conventional foliage decoration, usually embossed, adopted from the capitals of Corinthian columns and used extensively from the sixteenth century.

Beading round half circles, like a string of beads, most commonly used as edging decoration in the late eighteenth century, but also as a 'drop', when the beads diminish in size down the handles of 17th century tankards etc.

Bright cut engraving popular from c. 1790; a bevelled cut that removes metal, polishing as it does so.

Caryatid handles thumbpieces cast in form of classic draped females, surmounting handles on some early bowls and cups.

Coffin ended spoons the wide end narrowed by in-sloping cuts, exactly as with a coffin.

Cut card work decoration cut from sheet silver, usually as foliage or strapwork, soldered on to silver as applied decoration in relief after mid-seventeenth century, also serving to strengthen the metal at the joints.

Fiddle pattern violin shouldered stem to a spoon, early nineteenth century.

Finial the ornament at the tip of a spoon or on a cover, tooled to shape, or more often, cast in a mould.

A compote bowl by Tiffany and Co., New York; c. 1854–5. The base shows an excellent example of a key pattern border, the bowl is engraved with armorials and the decoration is applied. Although better known for their Art Nouveau-style wares, Tiffany's made an important contribution to American silver design throughout the Victorian period.

Flanged lid a flat projection.

Gadrooning a lobed border, giving an indented effect, spiral or straight, of any narrow width.

Meander wire an ornamental wire applied around the moulded base band on early New York tankards, below a rim of stamped ornament.

Patina the outer skin on silver formed through centuries of care.

Strapwork often interlaced ribbons forming panels filled with foliage or scrolls; engraved or flat chased in the sixteenth century.

Trifid spoons have a flat, three-toed terminal, sometimes with the ends turning upwards. Late seventeenth century.

Styles in Their Periods

Styles sometimes had the same names at different periods in England and America, but where the names are totally different the English has been used.

England	America
William and Mary 1689–1702	1685–1720
Queen Anne (with early Georgian) 1700–27	1720–50
Mid-Georgian 1728–70	(Chippendale) 1750–85
Neo-Classic (or Adam) 1760–1800	1783–1815
Regency 1800–30	1815–40 (Empire)
Victorian 1830–1900	c. 1840–1900
Art Nouveau c. 1870–1920	c. 1875–1920

ABOVE *An American covered jug made in Baltimore; c. 1834.*

BELOW *An en cage snuff box made in Dresden in the 1750s. The repoussé-chased gold mounts cover panels of mother-of-pearl.*

OPPOSITE *A collection of vinaigrettes in silver, gold and porcelain, late eighteenth and early nineteenth century.*

Pottery and Porcelain

Pottery is the name for anything made of common clay – earthenware – and which is allowed to dry in the heat of the sun or baked – fired – in a kiln. It is usually porous unless glazed, and is opaque, so that not even a strong light can pass through it.

Stoneware is very hard pottery, which is fired at a high temperature and often 'salt-glazed' when salt is thrown into the kiln. However, at its best it is so hard and close-grained that it requires no glaze to be water-tight, and can even be cut on a wheel like flint glass. It is usually opaque, but can be sometimes semi-translucent.

Porcelain (hard-paste) is the 'true' porcelain, which was made first in China and later in Europe by mixing china clay (kaolin) with rotten china rock (*petuntse*) and firing it at a very high temperature (about 1,450°C). It is very hard in texture and, usually, in appearance. It is translucent except when used in a solid mass, as for figures.

Porcelain (soft-paste) is 'false' porcelain made by adding materials *other* than china rock to china clay; in England bone-ash and soap-rock were added, while glass substances were used on the Continent. Fired at lower temperatures than hard-paste, it is translucent to varying degrees.

Bone China is an English modification of hard-paste made by the addition of bone-ash to the formula, and has been in general use in Britain since the early nineteenth century. It is a stable material and consistently translucent.

Glaze is a glassy coating applied to the surface of a pot by dipping or brushing on and it can be either clear or coloured. In the Far East, the glaze was usually applied to the pot after it had dried naturally (leather-dry) but *before* the first firing. In the West, it was applied *after* the first or biscuit firing. Unglazed porcelain is thus known as biscuit or *bisque*, and when enamel colours are painted directly on to the unglazed body the process is termed 'enamelling on the biscuit'.

Under-glaze and over-glaze: if the pot is to be glazed, the range of colours that can be applied before glazing is limited to those which will withstand the temperature necessary to vitrify the glaze. Painting in these colours, of which the commonest is cobalt blue, is called under-glaze decoration. A far wider range of enamel colours, and gilding, can be applied over the glaze, after the first firing, and are then burnt in at a relatively low temperature that does not harm them.

Vase and cover, made by Wedgwood in jasper ware. The applied reliefs in Neo-Classical style were designed to contrast with the coloured, unglazed stoneware body.

Marks: many collectors are obsessed with marks, but though of great interest and usefulness, they are not always reliable evidence as the pirating and forging of them has been only too prevalent a practice for centuries past. Until well into the nineteenth century, only a few European factories were at all consistent with their systems of marking, and a great many first-class pieces have no marks whatsoever.

POTTERY

'Tin-glazed' Wares – Maiolica, Faience, Delft The Italian version is known as *Maiolica* owing to an early misunderstanding. Spanish-Moorish pottery of the same basic type as the Italian, but with a metallic lustre decoration, was brought into Italy from Valencia on Majorcan ships, giving rise to the belief that it was made in Majorca. The name *Maiolica* has stuck to this day.

Between 1450 and 1630, the finest Italian Maiolica was made at Urbino, Venice, Genoa and Faenza, richly painted with trophies, arabesques, figures and flowers in a brilliant range of colours. This varied palette was forced into disuse by competition from the blue-and-white Chinese porcelain that was now coming into Europe, and which the Western potters had to imitate in order to survive. The sculptor della Robbia helped to raise pottery to the level of fine art.

French *faience* has much in common with Maiolica, borrowing its name from Faenza. It was made at a number of centres, the work of Rouen and Nevers in the late seventeenth and early eighteenth centuries being distinguished by bold modelling of such things as tureens, and confidently painted designs, both in colour and in blue-and-white. French faience, with an agreeable peasant flavour, has continued to be made at Quimper and elsewhere down to the present day.

Delft, in Holland, was devoted to the brewing of beer until about 1600, when its people's loyalties became divided between beer and tin-glazed pottery. The industry was highly organized into a guild which imposed strict rules of entry on its members, maintained high standards and kept a record of potters' marks which has come down to us, making the attribution of Dutch Delft that much easier. However, copies, complete with mark, abound. Most of the wares were inspired by oriental porcelain brought in by the Dutch East India

Company. Similar wares were made elsewhere in Holland and, indeed, in most European countries. In England, it was made at Bristol, Lambeth in London, Liverpool, and at Wincanton in Somerset. There was also at least one factory in Ireland. It all goes by the slightly confusing name, English Delftware.

Stoneware In Germany, the use of soft-bodied, lead-glazed or tin-enamelled pottery was largely restricted to stoves and tiles. A much harder ware, glazed by throwing salt into the kiln, was made at Cologne and elsewhere from about 1540,

being used especially for wine jugs with 'grey-beard' masks – popularly supposed to satirize Cardinal Bellarmin and known still as 'Bellarmines'. These were exported to England and elsewhere, complete with Rhenish wine; the earliest were white, the later ones brown, and the latest of all were grey with blue decoration.

English potters were stimulated to compete with them, and tiger ware jugs with a brown-and-yellow glaze were made in the Elizabethan period. By about 1670, John Dwight of Fulham had produced stoneware of a very high order, hardened by the inclusion of calcined flint, which he mis-

The Vincennes porcelain factory, under the aegis of Madame de Pompadour, established its reputation with finely modelled porcelain flowers. These date from about 1748.

ABOVE *Earthenware tray made at Rouen in about 1710. French faience of this period, covered with an opaque white tin-glaze was frequently decorated in this symmetrical* style rayonnant.

Earthenware charger decorated with trailed coloured slips of liquid clay, made by Thomas Toft in Staffordshire in about 1680.

takenly claimed to be hard-paste porcelain. Busts modelled in this material are very beautiful but also very rare. Much more common are the Fulham jugs, made on the lines of the German ones and sometimes decorated with the initials and portraits of Charles II or William III.

Two Dutchmen, the Elers brothers, introduced salt-glazed stoneware into Staffordshire at the end of the seventeenth century, and also made an unglazed, close-grained, red stoneware of a kind used by the Chinese for teapots, which the Staffordshire potters copied.

There is a legend to the effect that John Astbury, who became one of the greatest potters of the early eighteenth century, learned much from the Elers by obtaining employment with them and pretending to be a dullard. Industrial spying of this kind was a regular feature of pottery and porcelain manufacture in those days. Later, he brought white clay from the West Country to Staffordshire, added ground flint to it and made a fine, white, salt-glazed stoneware, used extensively for useful and decorative wares, and easily distinguished

from lead-glazed wares by its texture, which is a little rough – often likened to the feel of orange-skin. It was used on many of the early Staffordshire figures.

Jasperware – the product for which Wedgwood is best known – was also a kind of stoneware, again without glaze. Classical figures stand out in white relief on a matt ground in various shades of blue, lavender, green and black. First perfected in 1775, these colours penetrated right through the background, but from about 1780 the stains were sometimes applied only to the surface (*Jasper-dip*).

Stone china was a toughened earthenware first produced in Staffordshire about 1805 as an economic rival to porcelain. Mason of Lane Delph patented his formula for 'Ironstone China' in 1813, and dinner-services, jugs with snake handles and other objects are still produced, bearing the mark in full. This type of ware was, in spite of the patent, made at many other factories both in England and America. During the years 1850–1900 American makers produced vast quantities, calling it opaque porcelain or flint china. Regardless of name, the body is always much the same, and the glaze is always a lead glaze.

Creamware This was an improved earthenware, very light in weight, the body pale in colour and the lead glaze creamy, which was produced in Staffordshire about the middle of the eighteenth century. From 1760, it posed a serious threat to makers of porcelain and Continental faience – particularly French. Wedgwood made a version that became known as Queen's Ware and Leeds is celebrated for delicately modelled vases, mugs and other useful and ornamental objects. Creamware was often left undecorated, but some pieces were painted with enamel colours.

. It was made extensively in America from

BELOW *Clock case made at Chelsea during the 'gold anchor' period, 1758 to 1769, named after the raised anchor mark used at this time. This clock case has many features typical of the porcelain produced at Chelsea during this period, namely the Rococo style, the scroll base, the encrusted flowers which project freely, the rich colouring and the gilding.*

about 1770, first at Charlestown and shortly after at Salem, North Carolina. Several factories for its manufacture were set up in Philadelphia in the 1790s. New York and Pittsburgh were to follow, with Louisville and Kentucky producing the last fine creamware between 1830 and 1838.

Transfer-printing There are many ways of decorating pottery; one which revolutionized the trade was invented at Battersea in London about 1753, and was soon in extensive use at Worcester and Liverpool. A design was engraved on a copper plate which was then inked, so that it could be printed on to a tissue and, while still wet, transferred to the piece of pottery. Early transfers were in black, on to the glaze, and slightly later, in blue, under the glaze. The method was used on a vast amount of lead-glazed pottery, the ubiquitous Willow Pattern being a characteristic example of this type of decoration.

Victorian Pottery As the industrialization of the Staffordshire potteries developed in the nineteenth century, much hand-work was replaced by mass-production methods. The figures produced in moulds from the middle of the century to its end, many of them representing popular celebrities, illustrate the decline from the earlier work of Astbury, Whieldon, Walton and the Wood family. These named Staffordshire figures are nevertheless much sought after today.

PORCELAIN

Meissen When Augustus II, King of Poland, succeeded to the title of Elector of Saxony in 1694, one of the first demands he made of his economic adviser Von Tschirnhaus, was for an organized survey of the country's mineral wealth in the hope of finding the materials necessary for making, first fine glass, and secondly hard-paste porcelain of the Chinese type.

In 1704 J. F. Böttger, a young alchemist who had claimed to be able to conjure

CENTRE *Vase in parian porcelain decorated with modelled passion flowers and made at the Minton factory in Staffordshire in 1855. Parian, a fine, unglazed porcelain body designed to imitate marble, was introduced in about 1844 and achieved a rapid popularity because of its smooth feel and fine modelling qualities.*

BELOW *Group of lovers, modelled in biscuit, or unglazed porcelain at the Sevres factory between 1770 and 1780. The use of this material was popular during the late eighteenth and early nineteenth centuries in Europe because the lack of glazing allowed the qualities of the modelling to survive the firing.*

gold from base metal, was placed under the supervision of Tschirnhaus. By 1707 they had between them produced a very fine red stoneware, and in the following year the first white porcelain was produced at Meissen. It was near 1720 before Böttger used china stone together with china-clay, to produce an even whiter porcelain than the Chinese – the first hard-paste porcelain made in Europe.

From 1720 a brilliant young painter, J. G. Höroldt helped to produce the many copies and pastiches of oriental wares so sought after by Augustus. Under Höroldt, Meissen prospered and the famous crossed-swords, adopted as a factory-mark in 1723 became known throughout the world.

In 1727 a young Dresden sculptor, J. G. Kirchner, was engaged to model large animals and vases but was finally replaced in 1733 by the famous J. J. Kaendler, who was favoured by the chief minister von Bruhl. Kaendler was now requested to design table-wares decorated with high-relief and figure modelling, such as the Swan Service made for Bruhl himself, comprising 2,200 pieces. But he is probably better known for his series of small figures modelled after the characters of the Italian Comedy, Harlequin and Pantaloon being the most popular.

For many years Meissen enjoyed a near monopoly of hard-paste porcelain manufacture in Europe, but it became increasingly difficult to keep the secrets of production safe, and many rival factories were to start, among them Höchst, Nymphenburg and Frankenthal. Meissen finally lost its place as the fashion-setter for European porcelain during the Seven Years War (1756–63), when the factory was occupied by the troops of Frederick the Great.

Vincennes & Sèvres The factory was started in 1738 in a royal chateau at Vincennes, moving to a new building at Sèvres in 1756. Despite the early start it was nearer 1749 before good quality wares were being produced in any quantity. Due to the high cost of production, the factory might have closed down in 1759 if Madame de Pompadour had not persuaded King Louis XV to purchase the factory himself. Up until about 1770 all Sèvres porcelain was made from a soft-paste, but from about 1772 this gradually gave way to true porcelain, soft-paste being finally abandoned about 1804.

The history of Sèvres is well documented, including the dates when the

Sauce tureen and stand in the Neo-Classical style, probably made at the Welsh porcelain factory established at Nantgarw by the much travelled decorator, William Billingsley. Famous for his painting of roses, Billingsley worked at Derby, Pinxton, Worcester, and established factories at Nantgarw and Swansea, making fine quality highly translucent soft paste porcelain. Despite the quality of the wares produced, Billingsley's factories were only briefly successful, and the business was sold to Coalport in 1822.

various coloured grounds were first introduced, the names of the painters and gilders, the type of decoration they specialized in, and the years they were employed. About 1750, the factory adopted the royal cipher (crossed 'L's) as a mark and from 1753 the letters of the alphabet were used to indicate the year, starting with 'A' in 1753 and ending with 'PP' in 1793, when the concern was taken over by the Republic.

As early as 1753, a Paris merchant was advertising groups of figures in biscuit-porcelain. The French were the first to leave their figures in this unglazed and undecorated state, a fashion later adopted at the English factory of Derby.

Chelsea Porcelain was not made in England until about 1745, when the Huguenot silversmith, Nicholas Sprimont, began to make soft-paste porcelain at Chelsea, in London, probably assisted initially by a Charles Gouyn, a jeweller. Chelsea falls conveniently into five distinct periods, four

of which are known by the mark in use at the time, though much was unmarked. The earliest, known as the incised triangle, dating from about 1745–49, is found on wares of a glassy soft-paste, with a good, clear glaze which rarely crazed. Many of the early shapes were similar to those previously made by Sprimont in silver, taking the form of small jugs, salts, sauce-boats, etc.

From about 1749–52, the mark of an anchor, raised in relief on an oval medallion, was used. In this and the following red-anchor period (c. 1752–8), the glaze usually looks distinctly whiter, due to the addition of a small quantity of tin-oxide. The designs were very rarely original, imitating first Meissen, and then Sèvres.

The table-wares of Chelsea can often be identified, irrespective of mark, by three little blemishes left in the glaze by the stills used to support the wares in the kiln. Tears of glaze which sometimes formed on the edge of the foot-rims, were often ground

Group of wares made by Wedgwood from his famous creamware, or Queen's Ware body, in about 1775, and decorated with overglaze transfer-prints. The fine, white, thinly potted earthenware that became known as creamware, revolutionized the English ceramic industry after its introduction in about 1765.

55

away, giving a characteristic ground foot-rim. Red-anchor plates, when held against a strong light, exhibit tiny moons of greater translucency than the rest.

During the years 1758–70 the majority of Chelsea wares were marked with a gold anchor – only too frequently seen on hard-paste Continental reproductions of Chelsea. In 1770 the Chelsea concern was taken over by William Duesbury, already proprietor of the Derby factory, who continued to run both until 1784, when Chelsea was closed.

Derby Prior to the establishment of a Derby porcelain factory by William Duesbury in 1756, a number of very interesting and rare pieces were made by André Planché, usually superior to the early wares of Duesbury's factory, where figures were given a Meissen-like appearance, not so apparent in vases.

The Derby factory did not adopt the regular factory-mark of a crown, crossed

batons and 'D' until about 1782. During the Chelsea-Derby period, many of their table-wares were marked with an anchor and 'D', either side-by-side, or in mono-gram form.

Robert Bloor took over the factory in 1811, reviving so-called Imari patterns with brassy gilding on a glaze which often crazed. The original Derby factory closed in 1848, the present-day Royal Derby Porcelain Company being established in 1876.

Worcester The Worcester porcelain fac-tory was established in the mid-eighteenth century, and is still in production today. A partnership was formed in 1751 which took over the factory of Lund and Miller of Bristol, who produced a fine soft-paste por-celain from 1748–52.

Worcester porcelain was usually of a very high quality, capable of standing sud-den changes of temperature without crack-ing or crazing. Apart from a small number

Liberty cup and saucer, made at the Union Porcelain Works at Greenpoint, New York, in 1876 to celebrate the American Centennial. Fine gilding and modelling, and the raised pâte sur pâte *decoration make this a good example of American porcelain at its best.*

of figures, produced about 1770, their output in the eighteenth century consisted of table-wares and decorative vases, many of which were decorated in only underglaze-blue. About 1765, they began to employ colour in a somewhat similar fashion to Chelsea potters of the gold-anchor period.

Bonnin and Morris The first success in America appears to have been at the factory set up in about 1769 in Philadelphia by Gousse Bonnin and George Morris, who claimed their productions were equal to those of the factory in 'Box (Bow) near London'. The group of wares now attributed to Bonnin and Morris are of a thickly potted soft-paste porcelain decorated in underglaze-blue. The factory finally closed in 1772.

Tucker Philadelphia was also the city where William Ellis Tucker first produced a hard-paste porcelain in 1826 for which he won awards in 1827, 1828 and 1831. After his death in 1832 the concern was run by a Judge Joseph Hemphill, with Thomas Tucker as manager. It closed in 1838.

The enamel painting of flowers and landscapes was of a very high quality, as were the romantic scenes painted in sepia and charcoal. Many vases, pitchers and dishes were decorated solely with finely applied gilding, sometimes including inscriptions and dates.

Bennington The factory of Christopher W. Fenton at Bennington, Vermont, produced Parian ware, similar to that made by Copeland in England, in about 1847, including the famous Greek Slave modelled by Hiram Powers. Blue-and-white porcelain and more rarely, tan or green-and-white, was made from 1851. The mark USP (United States Porcelain) occurs on pieces made from 1853–8, when the factory closed.

Plymouth, Bristol and New Hall The secret of hard-paste porcelain, that in England had proved so elusive, was discovered independently by William Cookworthy of Plymouth in 1768. He moved to Bristol in 1770, where production was continued until 1781, when the patent was sold to a group of potters to form New Hall.

The hard-paste porcelain made at New Hall was somewhat different and appears to have a softer glaze than that originally

used at Plymouth and Bristol. From 1812 New Hall went over to the manufacture of bone-china until closing in 1835.

Spode The second Josiah Spode, of Stoke-on-Trent, Staffordshire, perfected a formula for a typically English compromise between hard- and soft-paste porcelain, about 1794. This became the standard product, known as bone china, because of the high content of bone-ash. The firm was extremely successful, making useful and decorative wares of all kinds, from the simplest blue-and-white to elaborate patterns like the famous '1166' – richly decorated with gilt scaling.

After Spode's lifetime, the factory passed to Copeland and Garrett (1833–47) and W. T. Copeland and Sons ran it from then until the present day.

Coalport, Rockingham and Minton Coalport in Shropshire, and Rockingham at Swinton in Yorkshire made wares in keeping with the fashion for revived rococo in the second quarter of the nineteenth century. Rockingham were inconsistent in the use of their griffin mark, but we now know that they did not make all the cottages, or figures of poodles with 'shaggy' coats, popularly attributed to them. The Rockingham factory ceased in 1842, whereas wares are still being made in Staffordshire today under the name of 'Coalport'.

The factory of Thomas Minton is also still in existence. Starting in 1793, their wares have always been of a high quality.

Meat dish, earthenware, made in Staffordshire in about 1820. The decoration, transfer-printed in blue, was designed to appeal to the American market, where vast quantities of English earthenware and porcelain were sold during the nineteenth century.

Glass

Glass is an unusual substance. It belongs to a small group termed supercooled liquids, which means that it passes from the molten to the rigid state without a change of structure. It is also termed amorphous, because it is not crystalline in its structure, unlike the natural hardstone, rock crystal, which it otherwise resembles. Glass is made from silica in one form or another, usually sand, with the addition of a variety of alkaline fluxes such as soda, potash, and lime, and sometimes of lead oxide.

Soda glass is the product of sand and sodium carbonate; in former times this was obtained from the ash of plants growing around the shores of the Mediterranean, such as seaweeds, or the Spanish plant, barilla, which grows in the salt marshes near Alicante. Spanish barilla was employed in England to make soda glass in the fourteenth century. Soda glass is light in weight, and, when heated, remains plastic and workable over a wider temperature range than other varieties, lending itself to such manipulative techniques as those used by the Venetians.

Potash glass is sometimes called fern glass, or forest glass, because it was fluxed with the ashes of inland plants such as ferns, which yield potassium carbonate. It was especially employed in Bohemia (now Czechoslovakia). Somewhat heavier than soda glass, it passes from the molten to the rigid state more quickly, and is therefore more difficult to manipulate into elaborate forms. It is, however, harder and more brilliant, and lends itself to such decorative techniques as facet cutting and wheel engraving.

Lead glass, also called flint glass, to which lead was added in relatively large quantities, was first known in Roman times, but for all practical purposes it was a late seventeenth-century English development by George Ravenscroft. In its brilliance and suitability for facet cutting it exceeds potash glass. It is the heaviest of all glasses, and in the eighteenth century it was employed by Frédéric Strass to imitate such precious stones as the diamond in the making of 'paste' jewellery. It was also used for the manufacture of eighteenth-century English and Irish cut glass.

At a sufficiently high temperature glass is a molten, fiery substance, but as it cools it reaches a state between the molten and rigid states in which it has a treacly consistency. This is soon lost in cooling but can be restored by heating, enabling various

Wine vessel in the form of a nef (ship), Venice, sixteenth century. The nef in the Middle Ages was a model of a ship in silver, complete with masts and shrouds, which would be filled with sweetmeats or sometimes with wine, and placed on the banquet table. Specimens in glass are very rare and manufacture was probably confined to Venice.

involved, or of stone or metal. Moulding preceded blowing, and the earliest blown glass vessels were blown into a mould, free-blowing being a later development. In modern times machines have been devised for doing this kind of work automatically, especially in the manufacture of bottles.

Glass blowing is a technique that demands a high degree of skill. When glass is in the plastic stage it can be gathered on the end of a long hollow tube and blown into a spherical bubble. All objects of blown glass start in this way, and by judicious reheating and continued blowing a large bubble of this kind can be formed. By swinging it at the end of the blowpipe a cylinder is produced. In its plastic state glass can be cut with shears, and for most manipulative processes it is transferred from the blowpipe to what is termed the pontil rod (or punty).

On Mohs' scale glass has a hardness of 5.5. This is slightly harder than ordinary steel, but much softer than sapphire, ruby, or emery (carborundum), and, of course, much softer than the diamond chips commonly employed to cut glass. The diamond is used to engrave ornament on glass of all kinds, and for this purpose it is mounted in a holder and employed either like a pencil (line engraving) or a chisel (stipple engraving). The technique of line engraving is very ancient, but stipple engraving first came into use in the Low Countries at the end of the seventeenth century.

In Roman times hardstones such as amethyst and agate were carved by abrading them with the aid of small rotating copper wheels charged with emery. The same technique was adapted to the decoration of Roman glass, of which some remarkable specimens have survived. Carving relief ornament is termed cameo cutting; patterns cut below the surface are termed intaglio, or, in German, *Hochschnitt* and *Tiefschnitt* respectively. The German terms are often employed because some exceptionally fine work of this kind was done in Bohemia in the seventeenth and eighteenth centuries.

Allied to cameo cutting is facet cutting, which is usually referred to as cut glass. Lead glass is normally employed for this purpose because of its power of higher refraction and reflection, in which it resembles to a lesser degree a cut diamond. The patterns into which this kind of glass is cut often resemble the faceting of a dia-

manipulative processes to be carried out over a relatively long period of time, especially in the case of soda glass.

There are two principal ways of forming objects of glass – moulding and blowing. Moulded glass vessels are made by pouring molten glass into a mould which is in the form of the exterior of the desired object, the interior being formed by a core. If the glass is blown into the mould a core is unnecessary. Some of the earliest glass was made in moulds filled with powdered glass which was subsequently fused by heating, and this practice was revived in the nineteenth century in the manufacture of the glass sometimes termed *pâte de verre*. Moulds were usually made of a refractory fireclay able to withstand the temperatures

mond, and each face collects light and reflects it at a different angle to that of its incidence. The brilliance of cut glass is partly due to the faceting, and partly to the qualities of the glass itself. Lead glass has been employed for most work of this kind, particularly in England and Ireland.

There are a number of metallic oxides which have been employed since very early times to add colour to glass. Before the discovery that manganese could be employed to remove the unwanted colour resulting from impurities in the raw materials, glass was frequently coloured, and copper was perhaps the most favoured colouring agent. According to the manner of use copper yields turquoise blue, a shade usually known as copper green, and red. Iron also yields blue, but since the eighteenth century the most popular source of this colour has been cobalt oxide, which is also employed to colour pottery glazes and for underglaze decoration. Opaque white glass results from the addition of tin oxide, and the product is indistinguishable from the pottery glaze covering maiolica or delft. Glass opacified in this way was employed by the Venetians and others to make imitations of porcelain and maiolica. Gold yields a rose colour, and this metal was the basis of the seventeenth-century purple of Cassius. Chromate of lead, introduced during the early decades of the nineteenth century, yields a good yellow, and it replaced the earlier mixture of silver, lead, and antimony which had been used for this purpose. Iron, according to the manner of its use, could be made to yield green, yellow, and a brownish black. For the latter colour it was usually blended with manganese, when a fine dense black could be produced.

All these oxides, except that of tin, could be used to produce a coloured transparent glass, and the colours could be opacified by the addition of tin oxide.

The nineteenth century was the age of the chemist, when many new processes were devised and developed, some of which are described later. Generally, however, the principles of glassmaking remained the same, and a number of ancient techniques were revived. Mechanical methods were applied for the first time to glass making, and the moulds into which bottles were blown automatically often added decoration in relief of a kind which has made them popular for collections, especially in France

and America. Glass pressed into moulds was an American innovation of the early years of the nineteenth century. Press-moulding of this kind can only be used where the opening is at least as wide as the base. The mould is made with the desired pattern in reverse. A measured amount of molten glass is dropped into the heated mould. A plunger, which may bear an interior pattern, is brought down, and squeezes the glass into its final shape, filling the depressions in the mould as it does so. The presses were hand-operated until 1864, when the first steam press was patented. Patterns were diverse and more elaborate than could be achieved by cutting or engraving.

Glass in Antiquity From the time of the early Christian era, ancient glassmakers applied almost all known processes of the craft, except the decorative treatment of acid etching.

By about 1500 BC hollow glass vessels had appeared in Egypt, produced by casting or pressing ground glass mixed to a paste into hollow moulds, or by hollowing out blocks of glass. Small colourful vessels, predominantly blue and yellow, were produced by the core technique, whereby a molten thread of glass was trailed around a pre-formed core. A great revival of this technique occurred in 700 and 600 BC and most of the surviving cored vessels available to the collector date from this period and were used largely for ointments and cosmetics. Colourful mosaic and millefiori glass, made of composite glass canes, which were sliced, laid side by side and fused, were techniques known as early as 1500 BC, and were produced most prolifically from 330–323 BC until the third and fourth centuries AD.

Glass blowing is thought to have originated in or near Sidon about the year 1 AD and brought from there to Alexandria, which became a flourishing glass centre. The very first blown objects are probably the small club-shaped tearbottles, frequent funerary finds supposedly for holding the mourners' tears. They often show an attractive iridescence, a type of weathering due to long exposure to damp earth or air, and make desirable collectors' items since they may still be found at a reasonable cost of just a few pounds. Glass broke away from the confines of luxury ware and emerged as a material for domestic use.

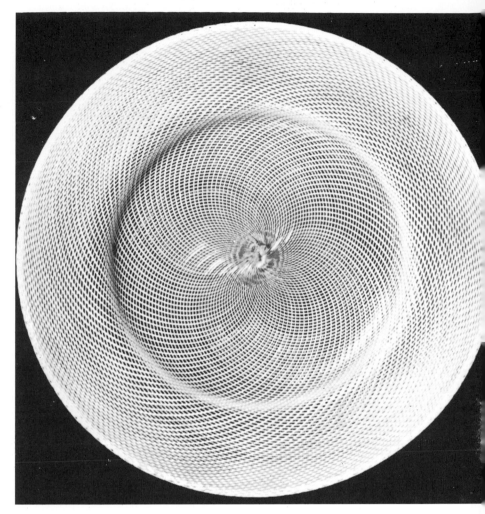

The glassmakers, travelling across Europe in the wake of the Roman legions, adapted their techniques to satisfy requirements for glass bottles and storage containers of practical use.

Nevertheless, artistic glassware was still made in the Mediterranean areas. Greece and Italy produced excellent cameo work, and this art was ably applied to the media of glass. The notorious Portland (or Barberini) Vase in the British Museum dating from the first century AD is one of the finest examples of early cameo glass.

The *Fondi d'Oro* technique was popular during the first four or five centuries AD. Here goldleaf is applied in the form of etched designs and sandwiched between two transparent glass layers.

The greatest triumph of the glassmakers art was achieved in the *vasa diatreta* – the cage cup (AD 100–300), produced by undercutting the outer part of the wall to form a network which remains attached by a few struts. The frieze around the upper half of the cup is carved to form the Greek or Latin inscription. Though most existing

ABOVE *Plate with folded rim decorated with white opposing spiral threads (a reticelli), Venetian, sixteenth century. This plate evinces a mastery of the technique which is unusual.*

OPPOSITE ABOVE *Claw beaker of green glass with blue trailing found at Castle Eden, Co. Durham, in 1775, late fifth/early sixth century AD. Blobs of softened glass were applied to the surface and then drawn out with pincers.*

OPPOSITE BELOW *Tumbler wheel engraved with a portrait of Prince Charles Edward Stuart, dated 1745. All Jacobite glasses are rare, but tumblers are exceedingly so.*

specimens have been discovered in the Rhine area, the effect is strikingly reminiscent of eastern ivory carving, and one might suspect some oriental inspiration.

Islamic Glass In AD 634, the Byzantine army was wiped out by Muslim forces, and with the rise of Islam a distinct Islamic style emerged also in artistic glass-making.

The finest achievement of Islamic glass art is the enamelling and gilding produced between 1250 and 1400 at the main glass centres of Raqqa, Aleppo, and Damascus. There is very little chance here for the private collector who must be wary of forgery, but the superb craftsmanship may be admired particularly in the rare fourteenth century mosque lamps displayed in major museums.

Venice To prevent further fire hazard to the city, the Venetian glass industry was moved to the island of Murano in 1291, still the centre of Italian glass-making today. The fifteenth century brought a revival of ancient techniques in millefiori, mosaic and marbled glass. Gilding and enamelling in brilliant dots and scale motifs is typical for this period, and enamelled figural representations found on deep blue or green goblets is associated in particular with the Berovieri family of glassmakers. The Venetian development of cristallo, a clear, fluid, soda-fluxed glass metal which cooled quickly and required great dexterity, revolutionized the entire concept of glass-making. Due to the re-discovery of decolorizing, cristallo was almost colourless, provided it was blown thin enough. It was therefore unsuitable for refiring, an essential for durable enamelling, but its fluidity seduced the gaffer to use all manner of fantastic shapes with trailed, applied and pincered decoration, often in a typical shade of blue glass.

The lace-like effect of latticinio glass was achieved by embedding white glass canes in a clear glass matrix which was then manipulated in intricate patterns. Shallow diamond engraving appears on cristallo

Irish helmet-shaped water jug, c. 1780. The helmet shape became fashionable with the advent of the Neo-Classical Adam style, not only for silver jugs, but also for those of pottery, porcelain and glass. Water jugs were commonly made by Irish glasshouses in a variety of shapes, but it is difficult to assign most specimens to a particular place with any degree of certainty.

this field were women – Anna Roemers Visscher (1583–1651) and her sister, with the Jacobsz brothers of Leyden and William Heemskerk, were the best known engravers in this technique. The peak of artistic achievement was attained in the stippling technique, whereby the desired motifs are engraved by means of minute dots applied with the diamond point or steel needle. The finest stipple engraving is attributed to David Wolff (1732–98). Existing specimens are all dated between 1784 and 1796, and the delightful putti and exquisitely dressed children typify rococo charm.

British Isles Glaziers from Normandy and the Lorraine came to Britain from the seventh century onward and were employed in supplying window and stained glass.

In 1676 George Ravenscroft (1618–81), a protégé of the Worshipful Company of Glass Sellers in London, succeeded in

glass during the sixteenth century, particularly on specimens made in England, Tyrol and Holland.

With the establishment of Venetian-inspired workshops in all important European glass centres, remnants of medieval domestic glassware gave way to more sophisticated vessels. Gay, enamelled decoration showed motifs of great variety – commemorative, historical, regional, domestic and heraldic – and was popular particularly in Bohemia and Germany.

The Netherlands The glass produced at the centres of Antwerp and Liège with the help of Italian know-how and workmanship is almost indistinguishable from the Venetian home product, and included latticinio and ice (crackle or frosted) glass of very good quality. A somewhat colourful revival took place during the later nineteenth century on the Continent, and in England. Much of it is of excellent quality and should not be scoffed at.

The finest contribution to glass art, however, was made by seventeenth- and eighteenth-century Netherland engravers who had sophisticated techniques and a highly original approach. Calligraphic engraving in the form of cursory script was applied to substantial drinking glasses such as the Roemer but is also found on wine-flasks of the mid- and later seventeenth century. Some of the most able artists in

Three eighteenth-century wine bottles, with characteristic mallet-shaped bodies and applied seals. Bottles of this type are clearly handmade.

developing his 'perticuler sort of Christaline Glasse resembling rock Chrystall,' and from 1677 his best specimens are marked with the Ravens Head seal, though crizzling, a defect due to excessive alkali content, was not entirely eliminated for some years.

Ravenscroft's success was obtained by the addition of lead oxide to the batch, and his heavy glassmetal has a unique watery limpidity and clarity of colour without the brittle hardness of Venetian cristallo, and excellent refractive properties.

The eighteenth-century drinking glass is a desirable as well as a precious possession. Styles are so varied that glasses are grouped and dated according to the features incorporated in bowl and foot design. The Venetian inspired baluster stem is one of the most important characteristics in English glasses between the years 1682 and 1730, and of Venetian inspiration too is the development of the enamel and colour twist stem, a most attractive technique practised from about 1745 to 1780. Intricate combined twists or rare colours in colour-twist stems will enhance both beauty and value of the glass. The stem with en-

closed airtwist was probably developed from the accidentally and later purposely introduced air bubble – or tear – and represents one of the most beautiful facets of glass-making, appearing first in trumpet bowl, drawn stem glasses about 1730.

The most elegant product of the English glasshouse is the Newcastle Baluster, a tall glass with a bell or funnel bowl, and, generally, a plain foot. Knopped stems often include tears and airtwists and bowls may show excellent engraving by Dutch artists.

Commemorative glasses of all kinds were popular during the eighteenth century. A special group is represented by the Jacobite glasses, recalling the rebellions of 1715 and 1745 with engraving of Jacobite symbols. The proportion of the drinking glass is an important guide for the collector. In the English specimen the circumference of the foot about equals that of the rim of the bowl, and the foot should rise at the centre to meet the stem.

English rococo is represented in the enamelled decoration seen best in opaque white glass produced mainly in the Bristol and Staffordshire areas. Michael Edkins

Wineglass with bucket-shaped bowl and air-twist stem, enamelled by Beilby with the arms of Buckmaster of Lincoln, c. 1765. William and Mary Beilby of Newcastle-on-Tyne are the best-known eighteenth-century enamellers on glass. William learned the art of enamelling in Birmingham with a maker of small boxes of copper decorated with painted enamels, and his brother Ralph was a wood engraver who specialized in heraldic subjects. As the signature on these glasses is simply Beilby, it is impossible to separate the work of brother and sister, but Mary was much younger than William (she was 16 in 1765) so the armorial glasses are probably almost entirely his.

(1733–1811) and James Giles (1713–80), though differing in style, belong to the élite of eighteenth-century enamellers and gilders decorating glass and china ware. In Newcastle, William Beilby (1740–1819) and his sister Mary (1749–97) produced exquisite work in white and coloured enamels, and the Jacobs family at Bristol fine gilding on Bristol blue table glass.

After the doubling of the glass tax in 1777, some of the best cutters emigrated to Ireland which was granted full freedom of trade in 1779. English-supported glasshouses sprang up in Waterford, Cork, Belfast and Dublin, producing heavy quality cut tableglass, and from 1780–1825 we may speak of an Anglo-Irish period.

In the later nineteenth century, the finest work was produced in the Stourbridge area where John Northwood (1836–1902) and the Woodall Brothers initiated the artistic revival of cameo glass techniques, and Thomas Webb's Company attracted many excellent Bohemian glasscutters.

ABOVE *French paperweight of the type keenly collected. This example, made at Saint-Louis in the 1840s, shows a mixture of marbling and millefiore techniques.*

LEFT *English leaded crystal Chandelier, about 1775.*

Bohemia Caspar Lehman (1570–1622), lapidary to Rudolf II at Prague, is credited to have been the first to apply wheel engraving to the brittleness of baroque soda glass. By the late seventeenth century, a more suitable glassmetal had been developed, and during the early eighteenth century an unrivalled technique in Hoch – and Tiefschnitt, akin to rock crystal cutting – high and low relief cutting had been evolved by Bohemian and Silesian glass artists. With commercial expansion, the influence of Bohemian glass art became world wide. Johann Kunckel (1630–1703) developed his gold-ruby glass at Potsdam and by the early nineteenth century Bohemia had established herself as leader in the field of coloured glass. Coloured, cut and engraved overlay glass became a Bohemian speciality and was exported – and imitated – all over the world.

France The most avidly collected and collectable French glass was produced during the nineteenth century. Baccarat created a brilliant glassmetal in fine colours, including uranium (fluorescent) glass, enriched by excellent cutting. From 1823 to 1848, the ingenious experiments of George Bontemps at Choisy-le-Roi in reviving latticinio and millefiori techniques, were instrumental in the creation of the famous French paperweight.

The three main factories producing this colourful extravaganza were Baccarat, St Louis and Clichy, and some specimens are marked with dates and initials. Millefiori and flower-weights were made by all factories. St Louis is perhaps the least conventional with reptile weights and often a characteristically flattened dome. Clichy favours a swirl pattern, Baccarat specializes in sulphides – enclosing medallions or such metallic or refractory material. This process (cristallo-ceramie) was ably exploited in England by Apsley Pellat. A star-cut base is a further Baccarat characteristic.

With the foundation of the Ecole de Nancy, Emile Gallé (1846–1904) created a new art concept, particularly in glass-making techniques. Emphasis was on individual studio work of great originality based on the fullest exploitation of the glass metal. The influence of Gallé's cameo-glass technique was enormous. Among the best exponents of the Ecole de Nancy were the Daum brothers at Nancy and Muller Frères of Lunéville. Brocard specialized in Islamic style enamelling, Cros, Dammouse, Décorchemont, Argy Rousseau and Walter produced most interesting specimens in *pâté de verre*. With the work of René Lalique (1860–1945), which ranged from exquisite jewellery to architectural fountains, and the powerful glass forms of Marinot (1882–1960), France has arrived at the very summit of modern glass art.

Carafe, ruby glass with a white overlay, decorated with cutting, enamelling and gilding, made in Bohemia, about 1840.

America The earliest glass-making attempts were probably made by English settlers in Jamestown, Virginia in 1608, and again in 1621. These ventures failed, and it was not until the eighteenth century that a glass industry became established on a successful scale.

In 1739 Caspar Wistar (1696–1752), a German-born brass-button manufacturer, established his glasshouse some 30 miles south-east of Philadelphia, appropriately naming the spot Wistarberg. Although the main output consisted of windowglass and bottles, tableware in the form of brown, amber, green, blue and turquoise vessels with wave patterns, applied threads and prunts, became characteristic of Wistarberg glass. Craftsmen from Germany and Holland joined the factory, which closed down in 1780. Under Wistarberg influence, a free-blown glass style of pleasing, bold form emerged, known as the South Jersey style. South Jersey glass was produced in attractive, clear colours, with amber, green and aquamarine being the most popular. A distinctive theme was expressed by the lily-pad motif, an applied glass decoration surrounding the lower half of the vessel.

Henry William Stiegel (1729–85), an ironsmith by trade, established his first glasshouse at Elizabeth Furnace in 1763, and by 1769 was owner of three factories in Pennsylvania. Glassworkers were imported from Germany and England, and tableware of good flint glass shows decorative enamelling in a rustic, continental style, well-suited to the taste of a German community. Mould-blown glass in colour with a preference for amethyst and a recurrence of the daisy in a diamond motif is associated with Stiegel-type glass.

Among these influential personalities, John Frederick Amelung (1741–98) was the only one who arrived on the American glass-making scene as an experienced glass-maker. When he came to the colonies in 1784, he was accompanied by 68 practical glassworkers engaged from various parts of Germany and Bohemia. By February 1785 he had established his New Bremen Glass Manufactory near Frederick, Maryland.

Existing presentation goblets and flasks in fine quality glass show expert craftsmanship and competent engraving in the Continental manner. Amelung's glass is probably the most sophisticated product of the eighteenth-century American glass industry, and it was unfortunate that due

to over-ambitious expansion and financial losses suffered at the burning down of the glasshouse in 1790, the factory was forced to cease operation after only eleven years.

One of the first glasshouses to produce cut and engraved tableware in English and Continental style was the Pittsburgh Flint Glass Manufactory founded in 1808 by Benjamin Bakewell and Edward Ensell, an Englishman.

In 1818 the New England Glass Company was formed by a group of Boston business men who had purchased the defunct Boston Porcelain and Glass Company. One of the partners, Deming Jarves (1790–1869) established his own factory at Sandwich, which was incorporated in 1826 as the Boston and Sandwich Glass Company. After Jarves perfected his practical glass pressing machine, the technique spread rapidly and revolutionized the industry throughout the world.

Early American pressed ware was usually of fine quality lead glass, and by 1825 a new style in glass design had been developed,

BELOW *Decorative lamp by René Lalique (1860–1945). It has a moulded opaline glass body and elaborate stopper with acid-etched decoration of peacocks on a plastic base.*

OPPOSITE RIGHT *Vase with violet foliate decoration in relief on a matt ground slightly suffused with violet, signed* Gallé, *by Emile Gallé, Nancy, c. 1900. Its very rare colour probably resulted from the addition of a tiny quantity of titanium oxide to the casing glass. Like so much of Gallé's work this vase exhibits a subtle but perceptible Japanese flavour.*

the so-called Lacy, produced by small dots in the mould. The stipple-pattern of Lacy glass has the appearance of textile or embroidery, and serves as a background to the great variety of popular motifs and designs. The best known objects in Lacy glass are the small cup-plates impressed with emblems, often of commemorative nature, and delightful salt cellars – small troughs designed in the French Empire or Rococo style, in clear colourless or coloured glass. An interesting collector's field is provided by mould-blown or pressed pictorial and historical pocket flasks, popular from about 1780, and made in several colours.

The Art Nouveau movement brought overwhelming response particularly in the work of Louis Comfort Tiffany (1848–1933). The company was established in 1878 and a number of unusually interesting glass techniques were developed due to experiments with metallic films and inclusions. Tiffany was fascinated by coloured glass and the art of stained-glass windows as well as the simplicity and irregularity of form of ancient glass. The most successful of his achievements is the *Favrile*, an iridescent glass in brilliant peacock colours. The influence of this concept is particularly pronounced in the Papillon glass made by Lötz Witwe at Klostermühle, Bohemia.

In 1864, a cheaper substitute for lead glass – the lime-soda glass developed by William Leighton of the Wheeling Glass Factory in West Virginia – spelled disaster for some of the manufacturers of fine quality lead glass and they were forced to close down.

The New England Glass Company ceased operations in 1888, and the manager, Edward D. Libbey, acquired the Charter and moved the company to Toledo, Ohio, where fine glass is made to this day. The Corning glassworks, reorganized in 1875 from an amalgamation of earlier factories, are now incorporated in the Steuben Glass Company who produce quality crystal glass.

Scandinavia has achieved an enviable reputation for interior design, to which the art of glass has made a considerable contribution. Though glass has been made in Sweden since the sixteenth century, its rise to contemporary esteem began with the founding of the Orrefors Glasbruk in 1915. Orrefors developed a kind of glass flashed with coloured stains termed 'Graalglas', and a school of glass cutting and engraving was founded.

Furniture

The names applied to furniture styles are a little like flags of convenience on ships: useful for purposes of cursory identification, but sometimes misleading. Even the most sophisticated designers seldom abandoned one style completely when replacing it with another; almost always there has been a transitional phase between one dominant mood and the next. The unsophisticated craftsman in a country town might adopt a mannerism years – even decades – after it had ceased to be fashionable in the cities. Many designs which appeared in certain places at particular times have in fact been borrowed from other places and times, often from the remote past.

Classical beginnings As early as 1500 BC, the Egyptians had developed the bed, chair, chest and table to a pitch of refinement that demanded a wide range of techniques and a variety of materials. Legs were carved to represent those of animals or, if plain and vertical, were braced with diagonal struts. The X-shaped support, which was to appear time and again in subsequent periods, was also used. Figurative and abstract decoration was painted or inland with ebony, ivory and semi-precious stones.

The Greeks adapted many Egyptian ideas in the process of evolving their own style, which can be clearly seen in paintings on their pottery. The X-shaped frame gained in popularity, while a characteristically Greek chair, the *klismos*, has legs which curve inwards – a shape which has come to be known as 'sabre'. Turning on the lathe was a method used for shaping the legs of couches. Typical decorative motifs were the palmette, in a formalized shape; the 'key' pattern; and the human figure.

The Romans took over the Greek style, making it grander and with greater use of metal and stone. Massive tables were supported on slab ends sculpted from the solid rock. Others, made of bronze or silver, were elegantly conceived with an emphasis on vertical lines. Decorative devices included the anthemion (honeysuckle), trophies of arms, rams' heads and idealized representations of the human figure.

After the decline of the Roman Empire in the fifth century AD, many of the traditional crafts fell into disuse in what had been the Western Empire. In the Eastern capital of Byzantium (Constantinople – the modern Istanbul), the tradition of fine workmanship was maintained, with the classical

American press cupboard in oak and pine. Essex County, c. 1675–95. The carved strapwork on the drawer-fronts and the split turnery are similar to decoration found on English furniture of the seventeenth century. The American style is readily recognizable in the retention of turned supports above and below, together with enclosed cupboards in both stages.

styles of Greece and Rome intermixing with early Christian symbols and the abstract patterns favoured in the Middle East. Saints were depicted within borders of foliage and animals, which were elaborately carved on ivory boxes or painted on large wooden cupboards. These cupboards form a connecting link between the Byzantine style and that known as Romanesque. The typical Romanesque sacristy cupboard is painted inside and out with lifelike figures of the saints in vivid colours. Sometimes they were carved with 'arcading' – rounded arches supported on classical columns. Similar arcading is to be found on boxlike chests; a vestige of Roman architectural grandeur surviving into the stormy Middle Ages, when political insecurity made the accumulation of much household furniture hardly worth while.

Gothic Gothic art, architecture and furniture has little to do with the Goths, the German tribesmen who overran a large part of Europe following the collapse of the Roman Empire and reached the height of their power in Spain in the sixth century only to lose it again early in the eighth century. Gothic was originally a term of abuse hurled at the architecture of the Middle Ages by a pupil of Michelangelo whose object was to advance the interests of the 'new' style (now known as Renaissance) at the expense of the old. The style he wrongly termed Gothic actually began in twelfth-century France and flourished over much of Europe, especially the north, for the following four centuries. It is now used to describe a splendid, soaring style typified by the pointed arches and rose windows of cathedrals, and found repeated in miniature on much of the furniture that has survived. Like the buildings, this is solidly constructed and elaborately carved with foliage, and human and animal heads. Panels are

often carved with what is called 'linenfold' – which was originally meant to represent scrolls of parchment. Typical pieces were chests of massive construction, often fitted with elaborate ironwork; high-backed armchairs with box-like seats; tables mounted on trestles that could be taken apart easily, and stools which were made on rather the same pattern, with shaped slab ends. Much Gothic furniture was of oak and now strikes a rather gloomy note, but probably most of it was originally painted in carnival colours. The Gothic style enjoyed revivals in the eighteenth and nineteenth centuries.

Renaissance In 1453, when Byzantium fell to the Turks, the centre of Christendom returned to Rome. With it came some at least of the skills which had been preserved in the capital of the Eastern Empire. These made their contribution to the growing revival of interest in the classical culture of Greece and Rome, which had begun shortly after 1400 as a conscious movement, led by scholars, architects, artists and sculptors, but which was in reality a reawakening of the classical tradition that had lasted, in Italy, throughout the Romanesque and Gothic periods. Between 1500 and 1600, most European countries benefited from the resurgence, and many of them made their individual contributions to furniture design. In Italy, motherland of the Renaissance, rich decoration in carving and painting was lavished on the most important piece of furniture, the chest or *cassone*. France produced some splendidly carved walnut cupboards and cabinets in which the classical column and pilaster appear, the panels of the doors being decorated with carved 'strapwork' or formal inlaid designs. The chairs made during this period were high-backed with columnar legs. In Germany Gothic shapes were retained but decorated with carving in the Italian style, inspired by Greek and Roman mythology, a favourite subject being the nude figure surrounded by entwined foliage, and grotesque monsters. This decorative style developed into a recognizable type known as Mannerism. English Renaissance furniture also retained a Gothic flavour, but made much use of boldly turned legs on tables and bed posts. Carving was richer and more fluid than in the earlier, more austere Gothic.

In general, Renaissance furniture, though it sometimes included religious motifs in its

French gilt chair of the Louis XVI period, c. 1780–90. The legs, no longer of cabriole shape, are carved with a delicate spiral in the manner of Sené.

carved or painted decoration, was increasingly secular and even pagan in spirit.

Baroque The Mannerist style of the late Renaissance was followed in seventeenth-century Italy and, ultimately, in most other European countries, by the much more involved Baroque style, which derived from the highly dramatic architecture and sculpture of the period. The human figure, for example, which had been neatly placed by the Mannerists at regular intervals, joined by bands of carved scrollwork, was now depicted in more lively postures, the limbs interwined with the foliage. The total effect in the more elaborate furniture is both monumental and restless, and indeed the greatest Italian makers, such as Andrea Brustolon, were famed as sculptors. Carving was executed in great depth. Hook-like scrolls gradually replaced the vertical line for legs, but where it was retained, the line was embellished with complex turning on the lathe. Baroque means 'irregular pearl', but most Baroque furniture is essentially symmetrical in design.

This is especially true of the French version, strictly disciplined under such designers as Charles Le Brun and Jean Bérain, while Daniel Marot in the Netherlands, Paul Decker in Germany, Johannes Indau in Austria and William Kent in Britain were among those who influenced the work of designers in other countries. Some of these virtuoso performers worked simultaneously in two styles. Kent, for example, as late as the 1730s, was designing Italianate furniture with a strongly sculptural flavour for his coolly classical Palladian interiors. As well as these grand products, there was also Baroque furniture of a simpler kind, with features that again became international. These included the spiral or 'barley-sugar twist', the decoration of flat surfaces with applied mouldings and split turnery and the increased use of inlaid decoration, not only in the solid wood but also as marquetry.

Rococo A reaction against the masculine pomp of the Baroque style began in France about 1715. No style can ever be said to be entirely the brain child of one man, but it was the designing of Justin-Aurèle Meissonier, an artist of Italian origins, and the cabinet-making of Charles Cressent that

A typical Shaker room, showing drop-leaf table, armed rocking chair, chest of drawers with drop-leaf top of lightly stained maple, and panelled window casing painted 'heavenly blue'.

73

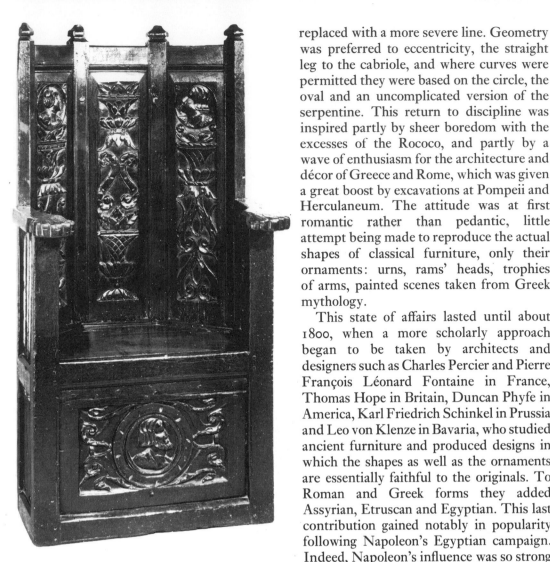

replaced with a more severe line. Geometry was preferred to eccentricity, the straight leg to the cabriole, and where curves were permitted they were based on the circle, the oval and an uncomplicated version of the serpentine. This return to discipline was inspired partly by sheer boredom with the excesses of the Rococo, and partly by a wave of enthusiasm for the architecture and décor of Greece and Rome, which was given a great boost by excavations at Pompeii and Herculaneum. The attitude was at first romantic rather than pedantic, little attempt being made to reproduce the actual shapes of classical furniture, only their ornaments: urns, rams' heads, trophies of arms, painted scenes taken from Greek mythology.

This state of affairs lasted until about 1800, when a more scholarly approach began to be taken by architects and designers such as Charles Percier and Pierre François Léonard Fontaine in France, Thomas Hope in Britain, Duncan Phyfe in America, Karl Friedrich Schinkel in Prussia and Leo von Klenze in Bavaria, who studied ancient furniture and produced designs in which the shapes as well as the ornaments are essentially faithful to the originals. To Roman and Greek forms they added Assyrian, Etruscan and Egyptian. This last contribution gained notably in popularity following Napoleon's Egyptian campaign. Indeed, Napoleon's influence was so strong that the period from about 1800 to 1820 is known generically as Empire, regardless of nationality. Its chief ingredients – the sabre-leg chair derived from the Greek *klismos*, the Greek-style couch, the circular table – lingered on as the Biedermeier style: severe in outline, solid, comfortable, middle-class.

Romantic revivals About 1830 the austere lines of the Biedermeier style were softened by a revival of the Rococo, especially of the cabriole leg. While some eighteenth-century designs were copied more or less accurately, there was also an unmistakably nineteenth-century style which, although it borrowed heavily from all past periods and mixed them up indiscriminately, nevertheless cannot be lightly dismissed. The general aim was usually to outdo the originals, so that proportions were exaggerated, lines distorted and decoration, especially carving, lavished with a curious lack of exuberance. This absence of spon-

led the way towards a lighter, much more feminine style that employed amusing idioms – shells, rocks, *chinoiseries* with a romanticized flavour – and delicate, curving lines typified by the elongated S-shaped sweep of the cabriole leg. If the Baroque was melodrama, the Rococo was light comedy. At its height, it reached absurdity but managed to remain charming, with a marked tendency towards asymmetry in the carving of mirror frames and the backs of chairs, and in the fashioning of metal handles and mounts. Marquetry decoration was used for floral designs, painting to depict the delights of flirtation in rural surroundings. Rococo was essentially a style for the boudoir, but as interpreted by Thomas Chippendale in Britain, and his followers in America and some European countries, it was definitely more cautious than the French.

Neo-Classical From about 1760 the curls and swirls of the Rococo were gradually

BELOW *Walnut chair, American, early eighteenth century. English influence is present in the basic structure and particularly in the shaping of the splat in the back, but a Germanic exaggeration of the Rococo style asserts itself in the asymmetrical carving of the cresting rail.*

taneity was inevitable when commercial manufacturers were putting together concoctions that included Baroque twists, Gothic arches and Rococo curves, all in the same piece of furniture, and using machinery for much of the work.

Honourable exceptions were the Gothic revivalist Augustus Welby Pugin and the medievalist William Burges in Britain; the executant of late Viennese Rococo, Carl Leistler; John Henry Belter of New York, whose Rococo intricacies triumphed by their sheer self-confidence; the Danish exponent of Neo-Classicism, Gustav Hetsch; Eugène Emmanuel Viollet-le-Duc in France, an architect and designer with a genuine knowledge of past styles; and in Italy, the creators of the style called Dantesque, who sought inspiration from the Renaissance for furniture, especially chairs, of fine quality, carved in walnut. Even the best of these designers, however, were nostalgic rather than forward-looking.

The Arts and Crafts Movement In the mid-nineteenth century principles of design and craftsmanship were expressed in the writings of John Ruskin and the Comte Léon de Laborde, who put most of the blame for the degeneration of taste on mechanization. An attempt to put their theories into practice was made in England in the 1860s by William Morris, whose workshops produced furniture of varying quality, hand-made and often fitted with hand-wrought metalwork. Morris was associated with the Pre-Raphaelite school of painters, and some of the finest furniture from his workshops, such as that designed by Philip Webb, is decorated with painted panels. Here was a conscientious attempt at creativity. Unfortunately a love of medieval ornament combined with a failure to make poper use of modern industrial methods imposed strict limitations both on Morris and his followers.

The Modernists On a rather different track during the early years of the twentieth

century were the inheritors of the Arts and Crafts Movement in Britain – Sidney Barnsley and Ernest Gimson, who produced good furniture by hand, mostly to special order, and Ambrose Heal, who designed in a dignified but more commercial way for his London store. The American architect Frank Lloyd Wright began experimenting in 1904 with stark constructions composed of boards mounted on frames. During World War I, a Dutch joiner named Gerrit Rietveld evolved ideas for abstract design in furniture, which were set forth in the influential magazine *de Stijl*, a name which has since been applied to the group to which Rietveld belonged. Many of their ideas were acted on after the war when Walter Gropius set up at Dassau in Germany a school of art and architecture, known as the Bauhaus. Here an appreciation of the lightness and simplicity of Japanese furniture was related to the needs of modern methods of production. One of the leading Bauhaus designers was Marcel Breuer, a Hungarian who pioneered the use of tubular metal frames. Experiments in this material had already been carried out successfully by Mart Stam and Mies van der Rohe of Holland. Though these experi-

mental pieces were hand-made, they led to the mass production of tubular and strip metal furniture.

The Swiss architect Charles-Edouard Jeanneret, better known as Le Corbusier, helped to found a magazine, *L'Esprit Nouveau*, and in 1923 published a book, *Vers une Architecture*. He declared, 'We do not believe in decorative art,' and in 1925 defined domestic 'equipment' as 'cases, seats and tables'. He began designing functional furniture in the following year, partly under the influence of Michael Thonet, a nineteenth-century Austrian famous for his bentwood furniture, and also of Stam and Breuer.

Alvar Aalto, born in Finland in 1899, first experimented with furniture in tubular metal and then turned to the beechwood forests of his native land for a material, laminated plywood, which could be bent and moulded to produce shapes in wood that would normally have been possible only in metal. All his designs are eminently suited to mass production without any reduction in the quality of the product.

Charles Eames, born in 1907, has been described as 'the first American furniture designer of international significance'. He

LEFT *Cabinet on stand, English, c. 1760, in the* Chinese Chippendale *style which relied less on painted decoration of* chinoiseries *than on architectural features like the pagoda top.*

RIGHT *Bed of the French Empire period, early nineteenth century, reputedly made for the Empress Josephine. The tester has been eliminated entirely from the design of the piece.*

was trained under the Finnish-born architect Eliel Saarinen, with whose son Eero he shared a prize for organic design in home furnishings in 1940. Since then Eames has continued to design furniture that combines elegance with practicality, and his work has been a major influence both in America and Europe.

It cannot be denied that this century has, under commercial pressure and popular demand, produced some of the shoddiest and ugliest furniture ever made in the history of civilization; but a growing awareness both of good design and the use of modern methods and man-made materials points the way towards a furnishing style of great purity and simplicity.

Wood Of all the materials man has used for making furniture, wood has always been

the most popular, in spite of the difficulties involved both in working it and in preserving it against the ravages of time and termites. Many other products, natural or manufactured, have been employed to embellish wood, and some have briefly challenged its supremacy. Nevertheless a widespread and deep-rooted preference for wood as a material constantly reasserts itself. Fashions for particular woods come and go, however, and vary not only from country to country, but also from region to region. Country craftsmen went on using certain timbers long after they had ceased to be fashionable in the cities, making out of solid oak, for instance, designs that were being executed in walnut or mahogany veneers by the master cabinetmakers in the great centres of production.

Veneering – the application of a thin

An American lowboy finely carved in the style of Benjamin Randolph of Philadelphia, c. 1765–80. Though related in design to the English Chippendale school, the filling in of the kneehole with a carved feature – in this case, a swan – is much more American than English.

sheet of decorative wood to the outside of a piece of furniture – is not necessarily a way of providing a poor article with a deceptively fine finish. True, it has sometimes been used to disguise shortcomings in the basic construction: in ancient Egypt, for example, the carcase was often built up with small pieces of wood jointed together, because large pieces were hard to come by, and the surface was then covered over with thin slices of ivory or ebony. Since the process was revived extensively in the seventeenth century, there have always been some makers who lavished their attention on the veneering of the exterior while caring nothing for the quality of the interior. However, veneering is a skilled process and the ability to practise it distinguishes the cabinetmaker from the joiner.

Chair made from the antlers of stags in mid-nineteenth century Germany. Many pieces of furniture were produced on the same principle. Hall stands were made from hunting trophies. The tusks of elephants were contrived to form tables and chairs, and even the animal's feet were made into umbrella stands.

Veneers are simply thin slices of wood, and all those cut parallel to each other exhibit an almost identical figure in the grain. They can thus be reversed and matched up to make symmetrical patterns that would be virtually impossible in the solid wood. The veneers used to be glued to a carefully prepared solid surface by a lengthy and difficult process, until the invention of the modern machine method of veneering plywood made a much-maligned material generally available to the furniture manufacturer.

'Oyster' veneers, popular in the late seventeenth century, were cut across the grain of small branches, or sometimes the trunks of young trees such as laburnum, displaying the annual rings. Set side by side to form a kind of patchwork, they really do look rather like a dish of oysters. 'Burr' or 'burl' veneers were obtained by cutting across the grain near the roots of such trees as walnut and elm. Other finely figured woods such as mahogany and satinwood yielded beautiful veneers when the logs were sliced across at various carefully calculated angles. Oak, whether used in the solid form or as veneer, exhibits its famous silver grain – pale, feathery markings – when riven lengthwise.

Different woods have often been used in combination by inlaying one into another of a contrasting colour. The earlier and cruder method was to inlay pieces of solid wood into hollows cut in a solid foundation. For example, sixteenth-century German chests of dark walnut were inlaid with designs in light-coloured woods such as box. Marquetry, developed in the seventeenth century, was the inlaying of a veneered ground with other veneers in different woods to make a pictorial design. Sheets of contrasting veneers, separated by sheets of paper, were lightly glued together before cutting the desired pattern through the entire thickness. When separated, the darker pieces could be fitted into the lighter, and vice versa. Each completed section of the jigsaw was held together by being glued to a sheet of paper, while the surface to be decorated was also given a thin coat of glue, which was allowed to cool. Then the marquetry design was laid down on it and a heated block of wood was clamped down over the marquetry, so that the heat melted the glue and caused the veneers to adhere to the carcase. Finally, the surface was sanded and smoothed, and additional effects

were sometimes carried out with pen, ink and artificial stains.

Parquetry was the building up of geometric patterns – as distinct from the pictorial designs of marquetry – by laying small squares of contrasting veneers edge to edge. By skilful manipulation of colour and grain, an optical illusion of three-dimensional perspective could be created. One variation, which originated in Italy but was popularized at Tunbridge Wells in England, was to glue together a number of lengths of wood, undyed but strongly contrasting in colour, to form a solid block. It was known as Tunbridge ware and developed in the late eighteenth century. This was cut into thin slices, which could either be placed side by side to form a geometric pattern resembling parquetry or arranged to make a pictorial design as in marquetry.

The designs used for marquetry and parquetry have employed many subjects. Flower and plant forms were popular in the late seventeenth century. Delicate, leafy scrolls, symmetrically arranged, are known as 'seaweed' marquetry. From the sixteenth century onwards Italian tarsia or intarsia combined both pictorial and geo-

metrical inlays to achieve remarkably vivid landscapes with buildings. A similar technique was employed in Germany. Floral and *chinoiserie* designs for the marquetry worker were produced by printmakers in eighteenth-century France. Between about 1770 and 1800 English cabinetmakers inlaid mahogany and satinwood with Neo-Classical urns and figures.

A simple but effective use of contrasting veneers is to band the edge of a table top or a door with a wood of a colour different from that of the main surface, and with the grain running outwards towards the edge. This is known as 'cross-banding'. It is usually emphasized by a thin line of very light-coloured wood (or in some cases black) called 'stringing'.

All these are methods of enriching the outward appearance of a piece of furniture; they are not in themselves indicative of the quality within. This depends on the kind of wood used in such areas as drawer sides, where hardwoods such as oak are generally preferred to softwoods such as pine; although many excellent pieces of furniture will be found that are constructed entirely of softwood.

Chaise longue designed by Le Corbusier (Charles-Edouard Jeanneret) in association with Charlotte Perriand and Pierre Jeanneret, 1927, and made of tubular steel. It is adjustable and gives priority to comfort.

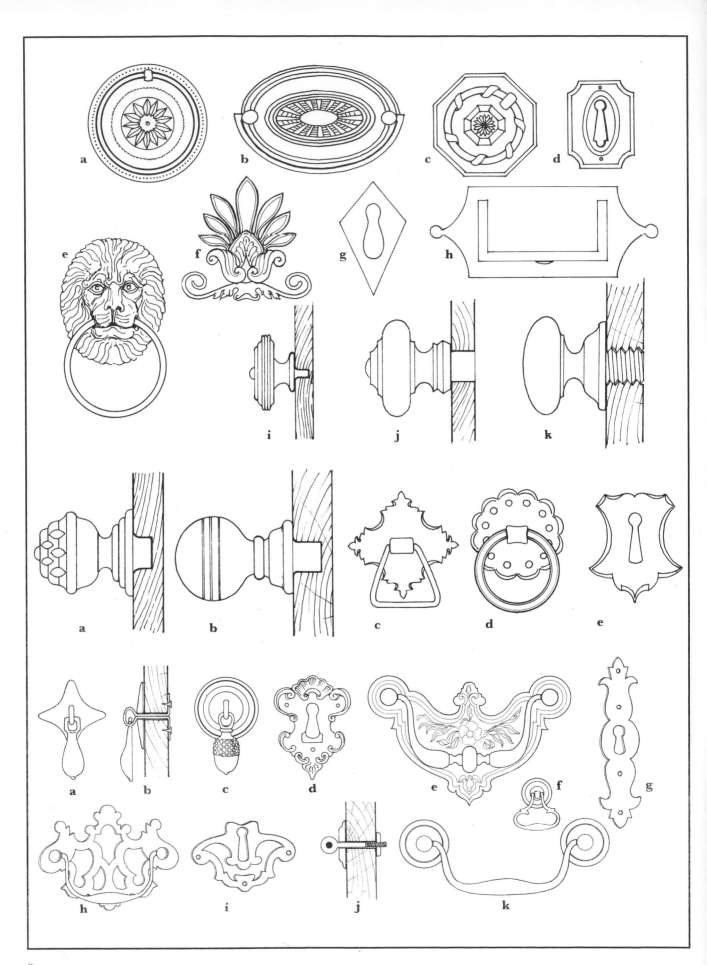

Handles and other accessories

TOP GROUP LEFT
Neo-classical:
1st phase 1760–1800
2nd phase 1800–25
a. b. and **c.** *Brass plate handles of geometric shapes, c. 1760–1800;*
d. *Brass escutcheon, c. 1760–1800;*
e. *Cast-brass lion's head handle, c. 1760–1800;*
f. *Inlaid ivory or bone escutcheon, c. 1795–1820;*
g. *Cast-brass mount based on Roman anthemion, c. 1800–25;*
h. *Countersunk brass handle, c. 1810–30;*
i. *Drawer knob in brass, wood or ivory, c. 1800–25; the dowel without threading;*
j. *Turned wooden*

drawer knob c. 1800–30; the dowel without threading;
k. *Drawer knob, wood, with threaded dowel, c. 1830–90.*

CENTRE GROUP LEFT
Gothic and Renaissance:
Fifteenth century to early seventeenth century
a. *Turned and notched wooden knob;*
b. *Turned wooden knob with incised rings;*
c. *Iron triangular drop handle;*
d. *Iron ring handle with lobed backplate;*
e. *Iron shield-shaped escutcheon plate.*

BOTTOM GROUP LEFT
Baroque:
Early seventeenth century to early eighteenth century
a. *Brass peardrop handle with star-shaped backplate, c. 1660–1700;*
b. *Peardrop handle shown in cross section with tang passing through drawer-front and secured with pins, c. 1660–1700;*
c. *Brass acorn drop handle, secured with tang, c. 1660–1700;*
d. *Brass escutcheon plate, c. 1660–1700;*
e. *Brass handle with pendant loop and engraved backplate, c. 1710–30;*

f. *Miniature 'Dutch drop' handle used on small drawers and bearers, c. 1710–60;*
g. *Brass escutcheon for cupboard door, c. 1730–50;*
h. *Brass handle with pendant loop and fretted backplate, c. 1725–40;*
i. *Brass escutcheon for drawer, c. 1730–50;*
j. *Method of securing handle with nut and bolt, replacing tang method, c. 1710;*
k. *Brass loop handle discarding solid backplate in favour of pair of roses, c. 1750–75.*

RIGHT *The French immigrant Charles-Honoré Lannuier made this American card table about 1815. The winged caryatid (female figures who serves as table support), colonnettes and hocked legs are painted black and partly gilt. Round the edge of the folding top of bird's-eye maple are inlaid brass stars, circles and anthemia. The inside of the top is veneered with satinwood.*

Clocks and Watches

It is interesting first of all to notice that the influence of clock and watch makers in the early years of time pieces extended well beyond this particular field. Interest in horology is international, and there are beautiful clocks and watches from every part of the world.

All distinguished people in the horological world working between the 1500s and the 1800s were craftsmen and some were scientists and philosophers. In the City of London for example, George Graham (1673–1751), nephew of the great Thomas Tompion, was elected a member of the Royal Society and was among the first to devise a clock showing sideral time (that is, time as indicated by the positions of the stars in the heavens) linked with a telescope. The first 'transit' clock at Greenwich, on which Greenwich Mean Time was based, was built by George Graham.

In Paris, Abraham-Louis Breguet (1747–1823) was among several distinguished horologists working for Louis XVI's court at his *atelier* on the Quai de l'Horloge. He was busy on a new watch for Queen Marie-Antoinette in June 1793 at the onset of the Terror. Marat sent secretly to the Quai de l'Horloge warning Breguet he was on the list to be guillotined, and must get away.

Breguet and his family fled to safety in Switzerland, returning to Paris after the holocaust to experiment in many advanced spheres of horology including decimal-time clocks, and calendars starting not in the 1790s but at 'Year One of the Republic'. Because of his brilliant horological work, particularly in precision pocket watches, most clocks and watches extant bearing his name (which was widely forged, even in his own time) are extremely valuable and sought-after pieces.

At approximately the same period, thousands of miles across the Atlantic, Simon Willard was advertising in *Thomas's Massachusetts Spy* of 11 March 1784: 'Simon Willard begs to Inform the Publick that he has opened a Shop in Roxbury-Street, nearly opposite the road that runs off to Plymouth, where he carries on the Business of Clock Making in all its branches. . . .' The site of this historic early American clock shop is known: today it is 2196 Washington Street. Willard pioneered the 'do-it-yourself' aspect of clock-making, in an American age when vast distances had to be covered on horseback or by stage coach. So that poor farmers and others could benefit from mechanical timekeeping he produced kits of parts, selling them with

RIGHT *In the nineteenth century mantel clocks, formerly a luxury, became common-place. This example is French, c. 1810–30, made of ormolu, and the clock is surmounted by an allegorical figure of music, strumming a lyre. An unusual feature of this clock is its silk suspended pendulum.*

FAR RIGHT *Longcase clock with a ten-inch dial, by William Moseley, 1685. The fine marquetry case reveals that by this time the clock had assumed the status of the best pieces of furniture.*

the advertisement: 'Such gentlemen or ladies who live at a distance may have Clock Work sent them, with directions how to manage and set them up, without the assistance of the Clock-Maker.' By contrast, the famous Pennsylvania astronomer, scientist and clockmaker David Rittenhouse (1732–96) constructed what was probably the first astronomical observatory in

America, to observe the transit of Venus. In England, King George III had the now famous little white observatory built at Kew, in Richmond Park, to witness the same historic transit. What follows is a brief outline of the major styles of casework and horological design.

Table clocks The very earliest examples, from the 1400s to the 1600s in Britain, and to the 1700s in Continental Europe, are predictably museum specimens outside the reach of private collectors. Argument will long continue as to the origins of clockwork.

Table-clock styles As domestic furnishing became more civilized, the somewhat crude although decorative early German-style table clock gave place to a type with a dial which could be hung on the wall, or placed on a sideboard, table or (later still) a chimneypiece. From old German prints such as those by Engelbrecht we can see how the brass-and-steel table clock gave way to the vertical-dial, South German metal-cased clock, and eventually by the beginning of the 1600s to the wooden case style. Ebony-veneered cases – later walnut and pearwood – kept dust and airborne ash out of the movements of clocks mounted on a chimney breast in the age of roaring wood fires. The somewhat crude 30-hours duration, brass lantern clocks (also known as post or sheeps-head clocks) of the 1600s and 1700s did not need as much protection; but when cased movements with a glazed door were the fashion, far more complex mechanical movements were coming into vogue, so that by the 1680s there were table or mantel clocks of one-month duration, or which sounded out the hours at the pull of a repeat cord.

Present-day collectors tend to refer to all cased and glazed timekeepers as bracket clocks, but strictly this term must be reserved for those clocks that were produced with a matching wooden bracket for wall mounting. In England, table clock cases are usually of oak, veneered with walnut, ebony, various fruitwoods, or decorated with fine marquetry. From 1770 more cases were made of mahogany, solid or in thin veneer strips; by then the rectangular case was outmoded and arch-dial clocks were favoured, mostly with what are usually termed bell-top cases. This fashion gave way in the early 1800s to more austere arch-top cases (approximately 1780–1825), and to 'balloon' clocks with circular silvered or enamel dials; these cases are sometimes of satinwood, with the customary fan or shell inlaid motif.

Mural clocks The brass-cased lantern clock was 'posted' – that is, hung by its hoop and spurs from one of the timber frameposts of the dwelling – but the domestic advantages of protecting the movement in a glazed-door case were soon realized. The hanging weights were unprotected, but a hood was placed over the movement. This fashion was of brief duration in England, ending about 1725. In Europe it continued right through to the mass-production era of the late 1800s.

Longcase case styles The longcase (grandfather) style reached its zenith in the hands of the great London makers, from the 1660s to the 1800s, although it must be said that the clockmakers were not casemakers. Indeed, craftsmen producing clockwork confined themselves to their designs and their bench work. They planned out and cut and filed their own plates and wheels, hands and dials, but they obviously used many different engravers and suppliers of small brass castings. It need hardly be said that in no case is the name on the dial plate the actual signature of the maker. Only a few tradecards and labels exist of casemakers who worked for the clock trade, and they were primarily clock-case makers working in their own specialist workshops.

In the Low Countries, Italy and in England, the earliest longcase styles were based upon quite small movements with dials roughly 8 inches (200 mm) square. Cases were usually of oak, ebony-veneered, and little over 6 feet (1.8 m) in height. By 1665 the 10-inch (255 mm) rectangular dial became standardized, and although all better-quality cases had an oak carcase there was a wide range of applied veneers. Marquetry panels, side panels of oyster walnut veneers, inlaid star and stringing or quite florid floral designs all had their run, but in London by 1685 the trend was to taller, more restrained casework in veneered, well-grained walnut without any stringing or banding. In 1695 a number of slightly larger movements were being produced, following the trend to build houses with higher ceilings. The 11-inch (280 mm) square dials of the 1690s gave place to 12-inch (305 mm) dials, and by 1710 an arch was added to carry a calendar or moon indicator, and of course this introduced fine new styles in arched-top cases. Some of the best are of 1775–90, when mahogany was still regarded as a new wood with exciting possibilities for the furniture designer. The first edition of Thomas Chippendale's *Gentleman and Cabinet Maker's Directory* contains some beautiful examples, and at least a few were translated into reality.

Few London clocks had dials wider than 12 inches (305 mm), and the trunk width was in proportion – seldom wider than 13 inches (330 mm). But in the provinces much larger clocks became the vogue – dials 13 (330 mm) or even 14 inches (356 mm) wide and these clocks can be very handsome pieces.

Metal cases Once the metal-cased table clock went out of fashion, most English and Italian makers showed a preference for wooden cases. However, for a short time in the mid-1600s some wealthy patrons demanded clocks with cases in styles derived from wooden models, but made of precious metal. One such clock was made to the order of Charles II by Tompion, and a now-unknown casemaker produced a magnificent case of silver, mercury-gilt. Among French makers, however, apart from a tendency in the Louis XIV period (1643–1715) to supply a demand for rather austere domestic clocks with architectural-style cases known as *pendules religieuses*, the trend

A small, green lacquer bracket clock with verge escapement, and a quarter repeat on six bells by Claudius de Chene, who was a famous maker of musical clocks. The case in particular is a fine example of early eighteenth-century lacquer work.

85

was generally toward cases of metal, or so decorated with metal – brass castings of caryatids and flowers – that they appear most colourful compared with the ebony-veneered cases of clocks in other countries.

Boulle, the decorative interleaving of fine sheets of brass, horn and other substances to form elaborate patterns, was created by André-Charles Boulle who was in fact one of Louis XIV's cabinetmakers, although he is sometimes spoken of today as if he were a clockmaker. Most 'boulle' clocks are in fact only in the style of Boulle.

The styles of French clocks of later periods follow furnishing fashions closely. The so-called Directoire era of 1750–90 saw a reversion to more simple clock styles. In the French Empire period (1799–1830) it was fashionable to have clocks and other domestic furnishings illustrating French military conquests overseas. It was one aspect of military travel that brought into fashion the type of French clock now so

much in demand by modern collectors – the *pendulettes* or travelling clocks, mostly misnamed carriage clocks. Rather stark designs were produced for French officers, and as the mechanisms were so reliable – a fine characteristic of most early French clocks – the style was followed by makers in Austria and England.

Watch styles Case design was of course controlled by horological developments of the mechanism, which we examine later in this section. However, by the 1550s small portable watches were developed in Continental centres including the Loire in France, and Augsburg and Nuremberg in Germany. The earliest were probably of South German origin, their makers working with early gunsmiths who had the necessary skills in steel and brasswork, and particularly in forming coil springs. The earliest watches had a single steel hand, and touch pieces were formed on the open dial so that the wearer could tell the time by sense of touch if the candles were not lit.

By the start of the 1600s what were known as 'form' watches became the vogue – the case no longer being a cylindrical drum, but shaped in the form of a cross, a skull, a peacock or some other device. Some were silver gilt, or had gold hands and casework decoration, while others were fashioned from rock crystal. By 1630 plain metal watch cases sometimes had the dial protected by a disc of rock crystal, forerunner of the later watch glass in a bezel. The crystal was held in place by metal tags, miniature enamel plaques came into fashion as part of the case construction, and although many silver cases were richly engraved in an anonymous floral style it is usually possible to distinguish the English from the Continental by the much heavier and deeper engraving of the latter.

Not until the 1660s did watches by London makers become more conventional in form, usually with a silver or gold dial and enclosed in what was termed a pair case, the outer protective case perhaps being decorated with tortoiseshell and silver inlay, or gold or silver pinwork. French watches of that period had a metal dial with the hour numerals let in, on enamel plaques. The white enamel dial did not become generally accepted throughout Europe until the first quarter of the eighteenth century. Plain and engine-turned silver and gold cases followed, and watches for export to

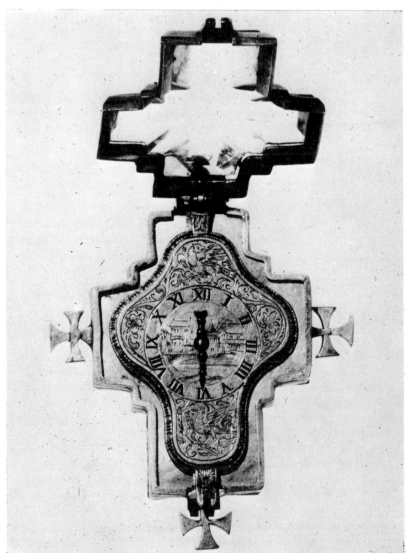

Form watch in the shape of a cross with hinged rock crystal cover made in the late sixteenth century, probably in Germany.

86

Middle East markets had florid engraving and decoration with horn or semi-precious stones. Soon after 1800, when the better makers were able to produce precision watches and pocket chronometers, plain enamel dials and stern blued-steel or gold hands were the vogue.

American Clocks and Watches Clocks made in America during the eighteenth century were European in style and were made mostly by craftsmen who had served their apprenticeship in England, Holland or Germany. Thus the clocks they made were either British inspired longcases with horned tops, or the *wag-on-wall*, with un-enclosed weights and pendulum, similar to the wall clocks popular over a long period in Holland and Germany. The work of makers such as David Rittenhouse, Benjamin Franklin, Thomas Harland, Thomas Claggett and Daniel Burnap is greatly sought after by collectors today.

It was an apprentice of Daniel Burnap,

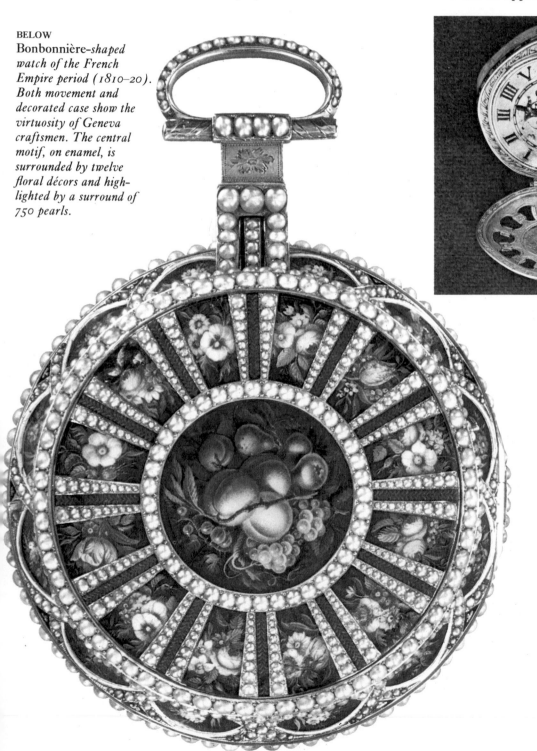

BELOW
Bonbonnière-*shaped watch of the French Empire period (1810–20). Both movement and decorated case show the virtuosity of Geneva craftsmen. The central motif, on enamel, is surrounded by twelve floral décors and high-lighted by a surround of 750 pearls.*

ABOVE *Early watches were sometimes set in cases of hardstones, such as crystal, agate or amethyst. This example, housed in a case of hollowed emerald, was made c. 1595 and is reputed to have been in the possession of the English royal family. It has a verge movement and there are half-hour divisions on the dial, which is unusual as there were generally quarter-hour divisions. The inner case is of brass-gilt, and the cover is pierced to reveal the numerals. The dial is of pierced silver, the single hand of blued steel, and the movement is of brass.*

Eli Terry, who revolutionized American clock-making. The Willards, of Massachusetts, are said to have invented the shelf clock, the first distinctive American type, by condensing the long case. It was Terry, however, who gave the new clock its own style and who produced it in quantity. His pillar and scroll shelf clocks were so called because he placed slender pillars on either side of the oblong cases, usually topped off with urn finials, and he also decorated the tops and bottoms of his cases with scrollwork. Below the dials of gaily

painted iron there was a glass panel painted all over with floral motifs or a naïve landscape, except for a circular area in the centre through which the owner could watch the wagging pendulum.

Originally, the movements, like those of many of the earlier American longcases, were made of wood. Only later was brass available in sufficient quantity to allow Terry to produce metal movements for the great quantity of clocks he turned out from his factory.

The pillar and scroll clocks were also

LEFT *French clock by Jean Trenchant in polished steel on a marble base. This is a radically modern design for a clock where the strongest effect is achieved by exercising the severest economy of design. Clocks were made of wood, chromium, silver, glass or marble; of any any material or design that would complement a modern interior during the 1920s and 1930s.*

RIGHT *A fine quality London-made brass lantern clock by Ahasuerus Fromanteel, seventeenth century. This ornamental descendant of the early iron 'Gothic' clocks shows the state of clockmaking before wooden cases became standard, partly the result of fashion, and partly to protect the more complex movements.*

produced in the factories of Seth Thomas and Silas Hoadley who had collaborated with Terry in the early days, and in a host of small workshops. They remained in fashion until an apprentice of Terry's produced a new type of shelf clock in 1825 to challenge their hold on the market.

Chauncey Jerome mass-produced tens of thousands of his bronze and looking-glass shelf clocks, undercutting all the other makers by selling them for upwards of 75 cents (30p) each. With brass mounts and looking-glass doors, these clocks were made in a variety of shapes, and were exported to Europe in considerable numbers in the 1840s before Chauncey Jerome's spectacular bankruptcy.

In 1802, Simon Willard patented what has been called 'America's most important artistic contribution in horology', the banjo

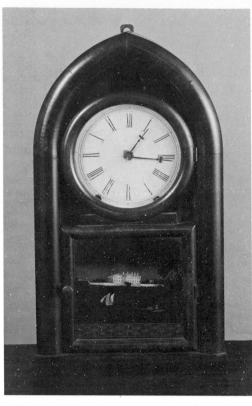

RIGHT *American mass produced clock, made by Brewster in about 1860. The gothic-style case has an inset glass panel decorated with a view of the White House.*

BELOW *American kitchen alarm clock, made by Elias Ingraham in about 1880.*

clock. This was usually fitted with high quality movements, consisting of a dial in a circular surround surmounted with an elaborate finial. Below this was a narrow trunk to which was attached a square box in which the pendulum swung, visible through a circle of glass, inset into the veneered front. Later these clocks were varied in design. The lyre clock which derived from French models had a gracefully curving lyre-shaped body below the dial surround instead of an angular one. They usually stood on a matching bracket instead of being attached to the wall. Another variation on the banjo was the so-called girandole which had a circular instead of a square base. This is the most sought after of all American antique clocks.

Unlike clocks, American watches are not very rewarding to collect. Of the few watches made in America before 1850, the great majority were based on European movements, and those that were not have little to recommend them. It was only in the second half of the nineteenth century that America made a valuable contribution to the history of watch-making, when the names Ingersoll and Waterbury became world famous, and the mass-produced American watch could be sold at a price that made it available to millions all over the world.

90

Mechanism No matter how beautiful or complex a clock or watch may be, it is a machine. A machine to tell the time. Power is applied – usually by a wound spring or by a weight – and as a result the hands are turned, and perhaps a bell is sounded. Other forms of power than those from springs and weights have been harnessed to driving clocks; the pull of a magnet, the variation of atmospheric pressure, and even the generation of hydrogen gas have been used.

In some watches and in most clocks there are two divisions for this application of power: the 'going' train, and the 'striking' train. Some have a separate 'repeat' train of wheels and pinions, so that by pulling a cord or pressing a button the mechanism sounds out the nearest hour, quarters or even minutes. When power is applied to the striking train, by mainspring or falling weight, the hammer would continue to make rapid blows unless slowed down by a small windvane at the top end of the striking train, known as a fly. The hammer would not sound out separate groups of one, two, three, four blows, and so on up to twelve, unless at the end of each predetermined group the gathering pallet had not completed its travel, a pin had dropped into a notch, or there was some such mechanical device to halt the striking.

The train of wheels and pinions beneath the dial is known as the motion work, and in former times clock and watchmakers were individual and ingenious in planting the train, so that an expert can sometimes tell the name of the maker without even looking at the signature on the dial. The vital matter, however, is what takes place at the end of the going train, for if there were not a mechanical device allowing the seconds to tick steadily away, the whole train would spin at high speed until the mainspring was unwound or the weight had completed its fall. This device is the escapement. It quite literally allows the power to escape second by second (at $1\frac{1}{4}$-second steps in some very rare English tall clocks of the 1685–90 period, and at 1/5th second in many modern watches). The quest for a near-perfect escapement has continued from the 1300s to the present day.

The earliest escapement one may hope to see on a domestic clock or watch is the curiously named foliot, the swinging bar or wheel oscillating over the spiked teeth of a

American banjo clock, made in 1808 by Aaron Willard of Boston. Perhaps the most characteristic of early American clock styles, these banjo-shaped pieces with their decorative panels are now highly sought after.

crown-wheel; most genuine examples are in the museums, although there was a revival later in Japan, when Dutch traders took old clocks out to the Far East. The ingenious Japanese found a real advantage in the swinging foliot (*esprit follet*) bar, for the positions of a tiny weight along the bar controlled its periodicity, making it possible to adjust the clock's rate according to the style of six divisions from dawn to dusk and through the night until dawn, which they had copied from the Chinese.

By 1649 Vincenzio Galileo in Pisa and (by 1657) the distinguished Dutch physicist Christiaan Huygens had devised a swinging pendulum driven from the spike-toothed crown-wheel, and this so-called verge escapement continued in clocks and watches until the next historic steps were made in perfecting time escapement. In the 1600s the London clockmaker William Clement (1638–1704) was the first to use the long 39.1-inch (approx 990 mm) 'Royal' pendulum, giving a one-second beat in a conveniently small arc, unlike the wide-swinging bob pendulum of the verge. The vertical crown-wheel gave way to the spike-toothed escape wheel in the same plane as the rest of the motion work, and above this is mounted an arbor (sprindle) carrying a curved piece shaped like a ship's anchor, giving its name to the anchor escapement. There are two tiny pointed ends, the entry pallet and the exit pallet, at roughly the same places as the flukes of an anchor, and these in turn are driven and locked by the movement of the scape wheel. By experts this is termed the recoil escapement, be-

cause if one studies it closely, or watches the seconds hand of such a clock, a slight backward-swaying recoil can be detected as each tooth of the scape wheel moves on. This makes for inaccuracy, and it was left to Tompion's nephew George Graham (around 1715) to reshape the anchor as the dead-beat escapement, virtually without recoil. An anchor-escapement clock can be heard to give a distinct *tick-TOCK*, whereas the precision-style dead-beat escapement is a quiet series of *tock . . . tock . . . tock*.

In watches, the early crown-wheel and verge oscillated a balance wheel, the movement of which was regulated (in fact made more accurately isochronous) by a balance spring. In the 1700s, with changing fashions in dress, there was a demand for a flatter watch than the so-called *onion*, and the cylinder escapement was devised, producing a much thinner movement as the escape wheel is horizontal, unlike the vertical crown-wheel of the verge. Graham's dead-beat clock escapement inspired his cylinder watch escapement (1725), and eventually we had the forked lever, the virgule, the rack lever (invented by the Abbé de Hautefeuille in 1772), the Chinese duplex, the double-virgule and scores more.

ABOVE *Gold watch made by Jas. Champion and dated 1779. Watches of this type would have had a decorative outer case as additional protection.*

RIGHT *An astronomical watch by the French maker J. Girond, c. 1660. The case is of richly chased silver. Separate dials show the hour, the day of the month, and the age of the moon. There are additional apertures for quarter-day, the date of the seasons.*

Jewelry

For thousands of years jewelry has been one of man's most prized possessions. Whether worn as a charm to protect against disease or danger, tucked away as an investment, purchased at great price to adorn milady's person, or in the market place of the poor for one's beloved, jewelry has become highly desired. Passed from generation to generation, it is loved and treasured in most intimate ways. It has sometimes driven man to commit crimes, but it has also brought joy and security beyond description.

What is in jewelry that has endowed it with such power? There is certainly something more than its intrinsic value, for many pieces of old and once highly valued jewelry have little material worth when broken down. What then is its power? Undoubtedly, it is in the eye of the beholder – a thing of beauty and joy, of love and attachment.

Classic Jewelry During Greek, Roman and Etruscan periods, jewelry was treasured principally for its gold. The workmanship was not especially sophisticated, the design was simple and appealing, but hardly the work of genius. Precious stones were rare or unknown at the time. Most of the impor-

tant gold pieces of jewelry are on exhibit in museums, and authentic pieces of importance are not too common in antique shops, though a few fine pieces occasionally come up for auction. Except for the cameos, most of the classic jewelry has little appeal for modern women. Even the elaborately granulated Etruscan pieces are roughly finished, and scarcely compare, for adornment, with similar jewelry produced by Castellani and other British goldsmiths in the nineteenth century. Classic jewelry took forms similar to modern jewelry, such as necklaces, rings, bracelets, brooches, pins and beads. Only diadems were singular to that period. Often they were placed on victors' heads at athletic events.

Renaissance Jewelry The first noteworthy period for jewelry was the Renaissance. The magnificent pieces created at that time were comparatively few in number and extremely expensive. They were made primarily for Royalty or for dignitaries of the Church. The middle class citizen did not use jewelry until the end of the eighteenth century. The finer pieces of Renaissance jewelry are now prohibitively expensive. There are still some lesser pieces available which are of interest to collectors.

A selection of decorative gold boxes, richly ornamented with painted enamel. These boxes reveal the variety of styles and tastes current in France and England during the third quarter of the eighteenth century.

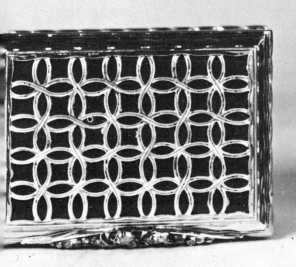

Hat ornaments called *enseignes* were very popular at this time. The fashion for cameo portraits was especially appealing to Royalty who had their pictures painted and set into jeweled frames by goldsmiths. Famous painters and architects created designs for jewelry with great pride. In the sixteenth century the robes worn by Royalty were studded with pearls and jewels. Enamelling achieved a high level of refinement, and the setting of a piece of jewelry assumed far more importance than the stones. Artistry in cutting stones had not yet developed and the backs of gems were still covered with gold or silver from the setting, but the reverse side of gold jeweled pieces was finished in a fine manner.

Eighteenth-Century Jewelry After the development of the brilliant cut, in about 1700, greater emphasis was placed on the gem stone rather than design and enamel work. Attention was given to bringing out the brilliance of gems, and most of them were set with silver rather than with gold. About this time the middle classes began to buy jewelry. Large pieces were being worn, especially with the diamonds set in silver *en tremblant* which moved with body movement. The gems sparkled in candlelight and attracted attention by their size and brilliance. The back of the gem setting now also opened to allow the light to shine through and enhance the stones. In Hungary, during the same period, enamelling still predominated and there was great emphasis on copying Renaissance pieces. Many of these Hungarian pieces are available and are valued as collectors' items.

Nineteenth-Century Jewelry Perhaps the greatest era of jewelry-making was that of the nineteenth century, particularly in France and England. But America also began to establish fine concerns around that time. While there were still many excellent goldsmiths in these countries who handmade outstanding pieces of jewelry, machine-made pieces supplied the needs of the average citizen.

Collecting Antique Jewelry Antique jewelry can be exciting, since not only is it beautiful and interesting, but it can be worn and admired every day and enjoyed as a conversation piece. It can also be a good investment if chosen wisely. Unlike the modern type sold in most shops, good

antique pieces do not depreciate shortly after purchase; rather they appreciate with time.

Most collectors agree that it is better to buy one good piece with whatever money one is able to spend than many small and inferior pieces that are less desirable. This applies whether one is buying a single piece to wear, or a specialized collector's piece. Most collectors buy antique jewelry to wear, while dealers buy to sell. Interestingly enough, the most serious and sophisticated collectors and connoisseurs of antique jewelry have been, and still are, men. They try to buy exceptional pieces for their inherent workmanship and artistic interest. These pieces are generally the kind seen as exhibits in museums.

Among the most eminent collectors in history are Medici (Italy), Gulbenkian (Portugal), Esmerian (New York), Gutman (New York) and Citroen (Holland). Most collectors of fine jewelry, however, prefer to remain anonymous.

Such a variety of jewelry was produced

ABOVE *Coloured gold and enamelled snuff box made in about 1820. On the lid is a portrait of Napoleon, signed by Isabey.*

OPPOSITE *A German buckle in gold and enamel and set with gems; early seventeenth century.*

in the nineteenth century that the fields open to both the wealthy and less well off collectors are endless. For most of us with limited means, opportunities for collecting fall especially in the following categories: shell and stone cameos, jet, memorial and hair jewelry, mosaic pieces, silver, steel, iron and paste jewelry, many of which have been unappreciated. American Indian, Mexican, turquoise, and coral jewelry is still plentiful and inexpensive.

Many collectors are interested in functional pieces such as stick pins, bracelets, hair combs, earrings, shoe buckles, rings, scarf pins and charms. Some collectors seek jewelry depicting animals and insects, such as dogs, butterflies, moths, dragonflies, beetles, and even gargoyle-like figures. One

ABOVE RIGHT *Enseigne or hat feather brooch. The front and reverse of this piece are thickly enamelled in bright colours of pink, red, purple, yellow and green. The rough cut diamonds are set in solid backed silver settings and having no sparkle, resemble glass. Such pieces were worn in hats, usually by men and they are rare. The enamelled flowers illustrate the popular liking for plants and gardens which was widespread in the seventeenth century.*

BELOW RIGHT *Two painted enamel mourning pendants and an enamelled pinchbeck buckle. The pendants are typical of late eighteenth-century style, when Neo-Classical severity was softened by sentiment. The pendant on the right has a frame of plaited hair. The finely enamelled buckle is a rarer example. Pinchbeck was often used as a substitute for gold, but the two can be distinguished easily because pinchbeck tarnishes while gold never loses its shine.*

BELOW LEFT *An English brooch of the mid-eighteenth century. The floral decoration is secondary to the bow design. The diamonds have the relatively new brilliant cut, but the settings are still solid backed. Open backed settings were not introduced until around 1770.*

of the most beautiful collections consists of enamel dragonflies and butterflies with moveable wings and inexpensive gem stones. There are also jewelry collections of lizards and monkeys, elephants and donkeys, seals, and pencils that elongate by twisting a top created with coloured stone.

One might even be interested in collecting English jewelry with an Egyptian motif, introduced by important archaeological discoveries in the nineteenth century; or with an East India look, made popular when India affiliated with the Commonwealth.

Collecting enamel jewelry is another exciting speciality, for countless pieces are available that are inexpensive but reflect much artistic design and craftsmanship. Collecting handmade enamel jewelry is an important speciality because of its beauty and delicate workmanship, especially if the enamelling is translucent. In England a special type called Jubilee Enamel was created to celebrate Victoria's 50th anniversary as Queen. The colouring is gay and glistening.

Another neglected field is that created by the Arts and Crafts Movement in England towards the end of the nineteenth century. Available in silver and gold, these distinctive pieces are of historical value. Small pieces of Art Nouveau are readily available and reasonably inexpensive.

If one has the means one might be able to collect the fabulous gold and enamel works of Giuliano or the finely granulated jewelry of Castellani, both Italians who worked in England during the nineteenth century. In the United States a few far-sighted collectors are seeking jewelry made by outstanding firms such as Tiffany, Marcus and Company, Caldwell, and Jenson.

How to Select Antique Jewelry Most important in selecting good antique jewelry is the assessing of workmanship. Inexpensive pieces are reproduced but not to simulate original pieces, because it is unprofitable, and it is not difficult to distinguish between a recent reproduction and a piece of jewelry made in the Victorian period. Generally, the reproduction appears new and unused. It shows the regular and finished edges that result from being stamped and put together by machines, and it shows also a high degree of finish. Stones are in an obviously machine made setting which is very regular around the edges. Inexpensive reproductions are not signed. If made of gold, a 14 carat mark is stamped on them, and they are quite likely to bear an American maker's mark.

It is always proper to ask the salesman or jeweler from whom one purchases a piece of jewelry whether it is new or antique. Then one can return it if it is found to be a

reproduction, bearing in mind that good pieces of antique jewelry appreciate while new pieces generally do not appreciate for many years. Important pieces of jewelry of all periods and styles are often reproduced and even signed with counterfeit signatures in order to command higher prices. Many dealers themselves are not certain about authenticity. Be careful, therefore, that excellent workmanship is present in an expensive piece of jewelry. Most good pieces are finished almost as well on the reverse side as they are on the front.

Prior to about 1850, comparatively few pieces of jewelry were signed, even if they were important pieces. It was only in the late nineteenth century, and especially by Art Nouveau goldsmiths, that jewelry was signed. In some pieces the signature was on the pin which may have broken and been removed. Or when a brooch, for instance, was made into a pendant, the signature could inadvertently have been removed. In jewelry made by goldsmiths such as Lalique, every fine piece was personally stamped with the goldsmith's name or maker's mark. Fine English goldsmiths such as Giuliano, Castellani, Brogdan, and Hancock, also signed most of their important pieces. Other goldsmiths, however, rarely signed their jewelry and purchasers have to be familiar with the characteristics of jewelry made by Ashby and Wilson or

Murphy, since they did not sign all their work.

In the United States, Marcus and Company, Baily, Banks and Biddle, Caldwell and Tiffany signed most of their important pieces and their signatures add prestige and assurance of fine workmanship.

Gold boxes The art of the gold box reached new heights, technically and artistically, at the beginning of the eighteenth century in the ateliers around the Place Dauphine in Paris, an area still known as the Quai des Orfèvres. Here thousands of exquisite little boxes were made to serve a new social habit, that of taking snuff, which became overnight the fad of a self-indulgent French court.

The golden snuff boxes which were made first in France, and later throughout Europe as the fashion spread from court to court, evoke perhaps more effectively than anything else, the sumptuousness of eighteenth-century court life. They are microcosms of that elegant age, which was at once intellectual and artificial.

The French snuff-box makers prospered despite opposition and legal difficulties in the early years of the eighteenth century. Not only was the king the avowed enemy of snuffers, but sumptuary laws designed to restrict the ownership of gold wares and jewelry to the court were still in force at the beginning of the century. Indeed the new edict of 1700 was more oppressive than those that had been earlier on the statutes, for it limited the amount of gold allowed to be used in the making of any single object to one ounce. This edict seems to have been often ignored, but it did result in the goldsmiths ingeniously using other materials for panels.

It was as a result of this edict that the *en cage* style was born. Slabs of mother-of-pearl, decorative stones such as agate, and later Japanese lacquers, were held in gold mounts, which varied from simple mouldings to Baroque frets.

The law was altered to allow up to 7 ounces of gold to be used in the fabrication of a snuff-box. As a result of this new freedom the 1720s and 1730s saw gold alone used increasingly to produce the intricately shaped boxes fashionable at this time. The surfaces of these gold confections were decorated all over with formal motifs, engraved, chased and repoussé. Bright surfaces were contrasted with those to which

the matting punch had imported a subtle texturing, and a rainbow of red, pink and yellow hues was achieved by the use of different alloys of gold for different sections of the boxes.

Boxes were designed to hold cosmetics, most of which, unlike the snuff boxes, had removable rather than hinged lids. Other boxes were made to hold a tiny sponge to refresh the owner, others concealed a tiny bar of soap.

Most important after the snuff boxes were the smaller and flatter patch boxes.

These held the snipped-out shapes of gummed taffeta which were applied to face and body. The positioning of these mouches, which took a variety of shapes – simple black dots, stars or silhouettes of insects or animals – was an art.

Philippe d'Orlèans, the Regent, had been a great patron of the boxmakers. He is supposed to have owned a different snuff box for every day of the year, but the assumption of power by the young king ushered in the great age of the box: the glories of French box-making for most people are the romantic boxes of the age of Louis xv. During his reign style followed style in rapid succession. Only a few of the more typical boxes of the period can be discribed to give, as it were, the flavour of the box-making of this long reign. French boxes now tended to have a simpler geometry than those made earlier in the century. Sometimes they are round, sometimes oval, but most of them are austerely oblong. To these simple forms, however, a riot of

OPPOSITE ABOVE *A typical mid-eighteenth century German snuff box, made from carved agate and mounted in enamelled gold.*

OPPOSITE BELOW *Mid-eighteenth century French watch case of banded agate, enclosed by a rococo frame of pierced and chased gold.*

A Louis XV gold and enamel rectangular snuff box, made in Paris in about 1750.

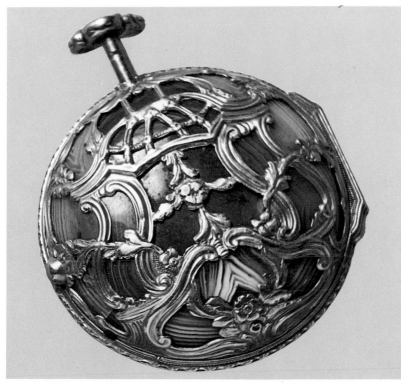

decoration was applied. To the tortoise-shell patch boxes Jean George made in Paris in the 1750s, for instance, he applied gold piqué decoration of an unbelievable delicacy and imagination.

The box attributed to Jacques-Malquis le Quin, which was sold at Christie's in 1972, and was made in 1749, illustrates another of the most popular forms of decoration of this period. The gold panels were given an engraved basket-pattern ground, and enamel reliefs depicting flowers and birds were applied to them. Around the edge of the lid there is the final and delightful touch of alternating blue and white, and pink and white ribbon motifs in relief enamel. Other boxes were heavily chased with figure groups, architectural motifs, birds and butterflies. Painted enamels reproduced the canvases of Boucher, Fragonard and Watteau. The use of the basse-taille enamelling technique – a variation of champleré enamelling by which the artist gave a subtle shading to the colours by varying the depth of the graved out areas he cut into the gold surfaces – produced some of the most glorious boxes of the period. The great makers like Ducrollay, George, Hardivilliers, le Bastier and Vachette among them, each had their favourite style, but all experimented in search of new felicities.

In the latter part of Louis XV's reign the Neo-Classical movement swept Europe and a new, architectural style influenced the appearance of all the applied arts, and was rapidly taken up by the fashion-conscious Paris boxmakers. On these new boxes circular vignettes were surrounded by heavy chased borders in which swags, urns and wreaths were frequently repeated motifs. This style continued in fashion throughout the reign of the weak and unfortunate Louis XVI, who died on the scaffold in 1793.

The Revolutionary period which followed was a thin time for the goldsmiths. A régime which encouraged the desecration of France's ancient royal tombs was likely to have little taste for such foppish, courtly bric-à-brac as snuff boxes, patch boxes and bonbonnières. But once Napoleon became securely entrenched as Emperor, he was only too eager to assume the trappings of royalty. The endless successions of boxes produced under his patronage with a chubby, seraphic and beribonned little Emperor flatteringly depicted upon them seem distinctly vulgar

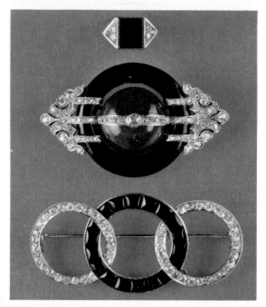

ABOVE *Three pieces of jewelry by Jean Fouquet. At the top, a ring in platinum, onyx and diamonds; in the middle, a brooch in coral, diamonds and onyx; and at the bottom, another brooch in platinum, diamonds and onyx.*

BELOW LEFT *Typical of the obsession with plant and insect forms, this brooch displays a bee poised on a convolvulus flower. It is made of gold and* pliqué à jour – *translucent enamels – and was made in 1901 by C. Dessosiers for Fouquet.*

Popular Victorian jewelry

LEFT TO RIGHT *Gold locket embossed with a typical Victorian pattern, a mixture of flowers, twisted wire and geometric design. Garnet bracelet with a machine stamped clasp. The oval gold locket is decorated with classical influenced granulation motif, framing a fine sentimental enamel miniature. The cameo is of lava, popular in late Victorian times. In the centre are two watch chain fobs, the one on the left is an engraved sard, the other a cornelian cameo. The tiger's claw whistle set in gold was a popular form of pendant after the British annexed India. Italian mosaics were at their most popular during the early Victorian period but they were still produced in the late nineteenth century. The fine green cameo in a gold seed pearl frame probably dates from the first half of the century. At the bottom is a fine jet locket, set with stones and a silver figure; on the reverse side is a compartment for hair.*

OPPOSITE

LEFT *The brooch is of gold set with emeralds, suspended below it is a baroque pearl whose mis-shapen form particularly appealed to the Art Nouveau designer.*

RIGHT *A more dreamlike face carved in glass, in a characteristic curved frame of gold.*

BELOW *The feeling of movement expressed in this style is well illustrated in the* pliqué à jour *gown which covers the form of a woman.*

103

and uninspired after the elegance that had gone before.

If the French were the great innovators and leaders of fashion, box-making was no French prerogative in the eighteenth century. Other nations, though they borrowed freely the ideas of the French, developed their distinctive national styles. Many fine boxes were made, for instance, in Britain – in Edinburgh and Dublin as well as in London.

In the first half of the eighteenth century British makers preferred the repoussé gold style, so popular with the contemporary watch case makers, and applied it to most of their rectangular, oval and bow-fronted boxes. One suspects, indeed, that both boxes and cases were the work of the self-same repoussé chasers, who with hammers and chisels raised and delineated intricate scenes of desporting classical gods and pert putti on the gold sheet. These chasers later briefly flirted with the alien rococo style, but usually without the conviction of their French counterparts.

A type of box which enjoyed a considerable popularity in England in the middle years of the eighteenth century was the étui, a slender gold case often oval in form, made to contain the accoutrements of sewing. Frequently, like the watches of the period, this was attached to a matching gold chatelaine which was pinned to the waist.

The typical English box of the reign of George III consisted of engine-turned panels between decorative borders – the turning usually of the barley or foxhead patterns that were to remain popular for nearly two hundred years. Sometimes these panels formed the base for all-over monochrome translucent enamelling.

In the eighteenth century the most important centre of box-making in Germany was Dresden, but later Berlin became equally famous after that most avid of snuff-box collectors, Frederick the Great, established a factory there and attracted artists from all over Europe to settle in the city. The Dresden makers specialized in *en cage* boxes, using a variety of decorative stones, deposits of which existed both in Saxony and in the twin towns of Idar and Oberstein – a cutting centre since the Romans discovered beautiful agates in the surrounding hills. The Dresden stone boxes took many forms, snails, lions, dogs' heads, pears and baskets among them. One of the outstanding makers was Benjamin Gottlob Hoffman, who produced delightful boxes to which dragonflies, butterflies, beetles and ladybirds carved from a variety of quartz minerals were cemented on to polished stone panels held together by slender golden frames. Another technique perfected by the Dresden makers was *Zellenmosaik*, a variety of stones being set in gold cloisons soldered to the box to create colourful mosaics.

The Berlin makers generally specialized in relief mosaic boxes, the materials the craftsmen employed for the applied reliefs including coral, lapis lazuli, mother-of-pearl and ivory. Plain enamelled boxes enriched with bold diamond-set thumb pieces were also a Berlin speciality.

When Peter the Great returned from his travels to build his new capital of St Petersburg, he encouraged goldsmiths from England and France to settle there, and laid the foundation of a great goldsmithing tradition which lasted for two centuries, and ended when revolution closed the workshops of

A selection of topazes. Topaz occurs in several different colours including colourless, pink, yellow and blue. The majority of topaz found is colourless and is called white topaz. The next most abundant colours of topaz are the blue and green-blue stones, which are similar to aquamarine. The colours most frequently seen in jewelry are shades of yellow.

the greatest of all the Russian boxmakers, Peter Carl Fabergé.

Russian box-making tended to be an admixture of external influences, grafted on to Russia's own Byzantine traditions, and informed by the Russian court's penchant for a richness that sometimes savoured of vulgarity. The chasing of the St Petersburg craftsmen tended to be more florid than French chasing, and diamonds were scattered over the large boxes which the Russian court seemed to favour, in profusion that exceeded even German lavishness.

Fine boxes were produced in Europe in the nineteenth century, and in view of the enormously high prices fetched by work from the best eighteenth-century exponents of the boxmakers' art, it may well be that collectors of modest means will foster the already growing interest in later work by being forced to seek for treasure in this less financially rewarding area.

About the genius of one nineteenth-century boxmaker at least there is no question. Peter Carl Fabergé made beautiful boxes in a great variety of styles, ranging from enamelled ones which have all the grace and panache of the great French makers, to those gold boxes with surfaces that look like volcanic landscapes, and that still seem avant-garde even today.

The Fabergés were a Huguenot family, who like many of their faith sought sanctuary outside their native country after

Louis XIV revoked the Edict of Nantes. Peter Carl's father, Gustav Fabergé, was a successful St Petersburg jeweller who enjoyed the patronage of the court, and was able to allow his son to travel and see in the museums of Europe the work of the finest goldsmiths of the past. When at the age of 24 he returned to Russia, and took control of the family business, Peter Carl Fabergé was steeped in the traditions of the eighteenth century, and his skill and imagination in translating them in late nineteenth-century terms, soon earned him a reputation which reached far beyond the country of his birth. A creation from his workshop rapidly became recognized as the most acceptable of gifts among the wealthy in every capital city in Europe during the latter years of the nineteenth and the early years of the twentieth century. His earliest work tended to follow rather slavishly the French models he had seen on his grand tour, but very soon he developed his own styles. He was always seeking, too, to widen the technical horizons of his craft. A patron who came to his large workshops to order a box could choose any one of 144 shades of enamel which could be laid over an endless variety of engine-turned surfaces. The same patron could choose from a whole range of exotic coloured golds, from greens to subtle pinks and rich reds. He also catered for the cigarette smoker of his day, creating flat and subtly curved boxes with the thumb-piece set with cabochon gemstone.

Two gold and enamel cigarette boxes made by Fabergé in a style that remained popular for many years, anticipating much of the Art Deco decoration that was applied to similar cases.

Textiles and Carpets

Samplers Test pieces of needlework provide a fascinating subject for the collector, and such samplers are still readily available. Their decoration and style are often interesting to the social historian, and their compact rectangular and flat proportions facilitate storage and display. They can be most attractive and decorative things to collect, with beautiful colours and extraordinarily skilled stitch work, and above all, many can summon up pictures of the worker and her life.

The word 'sampler' is derived from the Latin *exemplum* – a 'pattern' – through the old English *ensample*. The fabric on which a sampler is worked, the ground, is generally of woven wool, silk or linen, and the finished length was formerly determined by the width of the loom on which the material was woven. Other grounds, such as card and paper, were particularly popular in the nineteenth century. Samplers available to collectors today are, in the main, embroidered with cross stitch (*gros point*). Early 'stitch testing' pieces also used half cross stitch (tent stitch or *petit point*), eyelet stitch, satin stitch and long and short stitch. Some samplers were worked entirely in 'cutwork' (with the ground fabric cut out and reworked with stitching),

'whitework' (any white stitching on a white ground), or 'blackwork' (a monochrome embroidery, usually black or red on a neutral or white ground).

The history of the sampler can be traced back as far as civilizations such as that of Paracas in Peru. There are sampler-like designs on woollen textiles (Ross Collection, Museum of Fine Arts, Boston) from Paracas which had survived in the sands of that rainless peninsula from about 250 BC Somewhat less remotely, the sampler theme is found in the fabrics of Christians of Coptic Egypt from the fourth century AD Many of the countless fragments of genuine Coptic textiles in public and private collections bear evidence of 'trial' workings. Needlework made its debut long before the printed book and embroidery was a medium often employed to record designs and motifs. This was an important function of all early samplers.

The collector of samplers will, however, generally concentrate on more recent times. The earliest dated sampler is the 1598 piece by Jane Bostocke in the Victoria and Albert Museum, London. The intricate execution of the bottom and the comparatively open feeling of the top of this embroidery suggest that poor Miss Bostocke became slightly weary of her task! Samplers of the sixteenth century are, however, rare. Embroiderers of this period gleaned ideas from illustrations taken from nature, for Elizabethans were very garden-conscious. Tulips had been introduced to Europe in 1554 by Count Angerius de Busbeg, Austrian ambassador to Constantinople, and a passion for tulips is evident in most of the applied arts. Other flowers popular with

embroiderers included roses, daffodils and honeysuckle. Sometimes patterns were taken from contemporary herbals or from paintings.

Thus the role of the sampler evolved from pattern-recording to a method of testing the patience and dexterity of the artist. There is no direct evidence as to whether these early samplers were worked by adults or children, although they were

always from feminine needles rather than from those of the professional male embroiderers who were responsible for much of the embroidery of the sixteenth and seventeenth centuries.

Seventeenth-century samplers, with silk embroidery on a linen canvas ground, are recognizable by their elongated shape. A length was generally from three to five times as long as the width, which varied from six to 12 inches. Sometimes the finished work was stored around rolls of parchment or rods of ivory. Besides whitework and blackwork there was a lot of cutwork.

From about 1630 many samplers were signed and dated by their artists. Neat

workmanship, and constant repetition of some of the designs indicate that much of the work was done by younger needlewomen under supervision. Some early seventeenth-century samplers included sparing additions of gold and silver thread, either incorporated into the main design or added at the last moment, possibly as an inducement to finish the work. There were 'band' or 'border' samplers, with neat rows of patterns running horizontally across the cloth. And there were 'spot motif' samplers with devices literally scattered at random over the ground material.

The sampler repertoire often incorporates different stitching techniques.

An American album quilt, dated 1850, in which each square of appliqué design was made by a different relative or friend of the eventual owner. Most of the well-known appliqué patterns are included among the 81 signed squares.

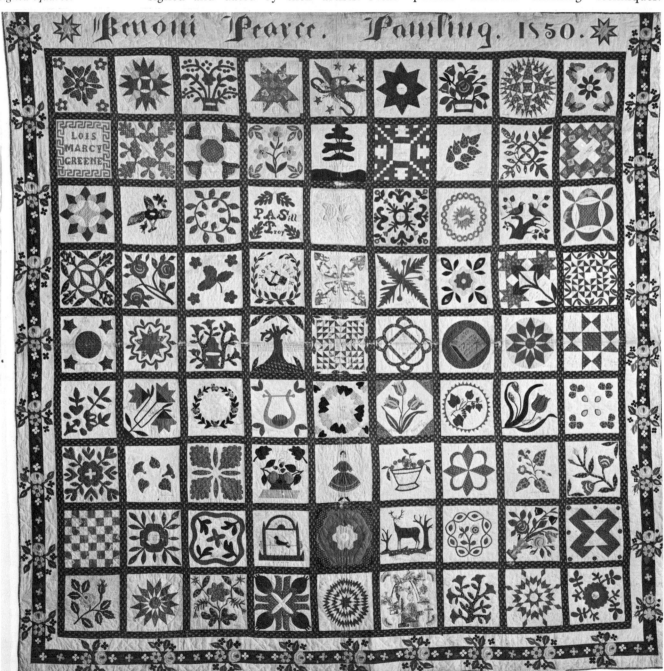

The earliest dated English sampler, made by Jane Bostocke in 1598. It is worked in metal threads, pearls, beads and silks on a linen ground.

American, seventeenth-century samplers, which were seldom worked by children, were long and narrow like those of European artists. But the New World embroiderers, more than their contemporaries, combined band work with cutwork and/or 'drawn thread work' (individual threads pulled from the ground to create a trellis effect). It is sometimes difficult to trace the pedigree of a seventeenth-century item, although some of the patterns incorporated into spot motif samplers may afford some clues. In the main, samplers from western Europe were closely interrelated.

The first half of the eighteenth century has been described as a period of transition in sampler design. Samplers of many countries were now worked with square proportions, and the move away from the close worked horizontal bands and motifs to new styles at the end of the previous century became increasingly pronounced. The scope of sampler art increased, as is evident not only in the subject matter but also in the gamut of colours and materials used. 'Tiffany', a glazed gauze, was used as a ground material from the 1720s to 1740s, and 'tammy cloth', a form of cheap woollen canvas, is found from 1780 onwards. Loom widths of the late eighteenth century were about 13 inches: American samplers were usually on a linen canvas ground and English ones were on woollen or cotton canvas grounds (the latter distinguishable by the blue threads in the selvedge).

Eighteenth-century samplers are often pictorial, with a carefully proportioned geometric or floral border surrounding the central subject. The overall design is usually balanced round a focal point in the middle.

Many of the pictures had a particular purpose, for instance the 'mourning

bet' pieces and the 'prayer' samplers. Sometimes one form of script was used throughout: sometimes different styles were freely employed. More imagination was being introduced into sampler production at this time.

In America, New England was a major area of needlework and particularly of 'crewel' or 'Jacobean' work, itself generally American in orgin. American crewel work can be distinguished by the use of 'Romanian' embroidery stitching rather than the more usual long and short stitch.

Interesting details of eighteenth-century life in America are revealed in many samplers. Girls' schools devoted much attention to needlework and many samplers can today be traced to the method of one particular school or teacher.

ABOVE *Detail from the tapestry panel* Love and the Pilgrim *designed by Sir Edward Burne-Jones for William Morris, and bearing the Merton Abbey monogram. Woven by Martin and Taylor, 1910.*

samplers', which have pictures and eulogies worked as tributes to the dear departed. They are primarily American, although there are some very fine English examples. They are generally worked in monochrome in fine silks on a silk ground, with memorial plinths and the ubiquitous urns and the weeping willows of remembrance.

Although pictures of houses first appeared on samplers in the eighteenth century, they are more prominent in the work of the nineteenth century. Familiar details afforded encouragement to the young artist, who must otherwise have been depressed by the painstaking work involved in the discipline of lettering, borders and signatures. She therefore stitched things associated with her life: her family, standing in front of the house, her dog, her toys, or a new hot-air balloon. These addenda give personality to the samplers of this time, many of which are technically not outstanding but provide much enjoyment for the collector.

Other popular early eighteenth-century samplers were the 'lettering' or 'alpha-

The nineteenth century saw the advent of 'Berlin wool work' and the consequent enormous increase in sampler work. Berlin wool work was conceived in that city in 1804–5 by a printseller who produced hand coloured embroidery designs on squared paper. (All previous patterns had been in monochrome.) By 1820, Berlin wool work designs were available by the thousand all over Europe and America. The ease of having the colours dictated with the pattern encouraged many who might otherwise never have discovered the joys of sampler making. The period 1820 to 1870, the heyday of this technique, saw an unparalleled production by needlewomen copying designs printed on loose sheets or ephemera, or from illustrations in magazines such as the *Ladies' Magazine*. Previously samplers

had been worked principally by children, except for the Dresden and darning pieces, but now Berlin work attracted a large number of ladies keen to follow the latest fashion. Berlin work was usually done on a ground of white open-weave canvas, and stitched in wools, silks, cottons with the occasional inclusion of decoration such as chenille, beads, beetles' wings and other exotica. The first aniline dye ('Perkin's mauve') came into general use about 1856 and, from then on, bright and even garish colours characterized the appearance of the embroidery.

The span of Western samplers therefore covers some 250 years. The collector will be fortunate to come across examples earlier than the mid-seventeenth century. Any 'traditional' types worked later than

BELOW *A French tapestry of the mid-seventeenth century.*

OPPOSITE *The Green State Bedroom at Holkham Hall, Norfolk, built for the Earl of Leicester from designs by Lord Burlington and William Kent after 1734. The room still retains the original Genoses velvets, the rich wall hangings and the heavily embroidered four-poster bed and furniture designed by Kent, and shows the contribution made by textiles to the Palladian style.*

RIGHT *One of a pair of English sixteenth-century gloves, presented by Henry VIII to his friend and counsellor Sir Anthony Denny. They are embroidered in red silk with gold and silver lace.*

1870 are not likely to be of great interest unless the work is outstanding. Collectors of topographical or other specialist samplers will not of course be confined within a particular period. Fine geographical and specialist samplers are being worked today. Whether they be by folk artists such as the Cuna Indians of San Blas or by a sophisticated Western embroiderer, may well achieve some value in time.

Tapestry and Embroidery The French Court in the eighteenth century derived much of its reputation for luxury and elegance from the tapestries made at the workshops at Gobelins, Beauvais and Aubusson. The industry at Gobelins and Beauvais, established in the middle of the seventeenth century to make expensive Flemish imports unnecessary, developed a rich and characteristic style that not only satisfied French society but also built up a considerable export demand.

Gobelins enjoyed state finance to produce tapestries for the Crown and so private commissions were only fulfilled to provide supplementary income. Beauvais, on the other hand, suffered from a shortage of customers, and so was financially unstable until the 1730s when regular orders from the Court began to arrive. The industry at Aubusson, whose traditions predated the other manufactures, produced a greater range of cheaper tapestries for a wider market, both in France and abroad. Tapestries were very expensive to make. After the original paintings or designs had been bought, these had to be converted into full-size cartoons. Then, after the purchase of the wools and silks necessary for the completion of the tapestries, a large staff of dyers, spinners and weavers had to be supported until the work was finished. Even the production of several sets of tapestries from the same cartoons only partially helped to spread the cost. As a result, many tapestries were sold for prices well under their production cost, and so State subsidies were essential. Frequently, tapestries were conceived as an integral part of a room's decoration, and so hangings, screens and upholstered furniture would be made en suite with the tapestries. In this way, some of the initial cost could be offset.

The Aubusson workers frequently assisted their colleagues at Gobelins and Beauvais, while others left to take their

skills to the Court tapestry manufacturies in Germany, Switzerland and Portugal. At Aubusson the lower standards of materials and design allowed for faster and cheaper production, and many Aubusson designs were either copied from Gobelins and Beauvais, or were based on popular prints.

By the latter part of the eighteenth century, Beauvais and Aubusson controlled the market, the one supplying expensive tapestries for the Court and the nobility, the other catering for the newly wealthy middle classes. However, the Revolution and the Republic that followed effectively brought the industry to a close.

Tapestry-making and embroidery experienced a considerable revival in England during the latter part of the nineteenth century. Prompted by the romantic medievalism of William Morris, a new tapestry manufactury was established to produce wall hangings from designs by Morris and the painter Burne-Jones. These greatly influenced the Arts and Crafts movement in England, while in Scotland the embroidery work of the designers of the Glasgow School revealed the powerful impact of continental Art Nouveau styles.

In America, tapestry never really developed beyond the level of a cottage industry. However, the American settlers of the eighteenth and early nineteenth centuries made an important and quite distinctive contribution to the history of textiles. The quilted or patchwork coverlet perhaps typifies most effectively the hard, simple life of the early settlers and, at the same time, is a quite characteristic American art form, whose styles reappeared in the paintings of the Pop Artists. The decorative patterns of these coverlets, with their charming and expressive names, can be associated with particular areas, and reflect, not only the strongly localized lives of their makers, but also the strong impact of religion. Many patterns can also be traced

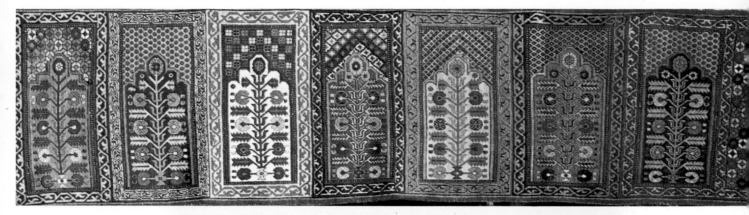

ABOVE *Samarkand Saph, or multiple prayer rug made in Eastern Turkestan, and marketed in Samarkand. Similar pieces were also made in Turkey. Generally woven from wool, or a mixture of wool and silk, these small runners were used for mosque decoration, for the compartments are too small for conventional use.*

RIGHT *Prayer rug made in the late sixteenth century for members of the Turkish Court, probably by Persian weavers. Its distinctive style and fine quality is typical of these Court pieces.*

back to the areas from which the settlers originally emigrated.

While produced originally for practical reasons such as warmth, and the scarcity of fabric, these coverlets are now highly prized, not only as works of art, but also as a vital part of American history.

Carpets It is necessary to define exactly what is meant by an Oriental rug or carpet. It is true that machine-made carpets and rugs are now manufactured in some parts of the East, particularly Japan, but the definition we are seeking is of a hand-made, knotted product, made in any of the traditional areas between Turkey and China. Some licence must be given, however, to include certain aspects of Balkan production, the early carpets of Egypt, and passing mention of Spain. Also included are the pileless fabrics used as hangings, divan covers or floor coverings, and known by various names, but most popularly as Kelims.

It is also necessary to define what is meant by 'rug' and 'carpet'. That is, a rug is any piece smaller than 9 ft × 6 ft (3 m × 2 m). From this size upwards the term 'carpet' will be used. There are two exceptions to this rule. A long and narrow piece is a runner, and a carpet of size 12 ft × 6 ft (4 m × 2 m) or larger, but in that proportion, is a Kelleye. The reason for this explanation is that in America the term 'scatter rug' is used for small pieces, 'rug' is used for large ones, and carpets refer to machine-made fitted carpeting with which we are not concerned.

The thirteenth century is the real beginning of the unbroken history of the craft, for although the next two or three centuries leave us little in the way of rugs themselves, and many of these not fully authenticated, it was an era of pictorial evidence, and countless paintings abound, particularly by Italian and Dutch masters, showing rugs and carpets as decoration either on the floor or thrown over tables. Some rugs have even acquired an artist's name, and one can read of 'Holbein' and 'Lotto' rugs, signifying the design painted by these artists.

Early in the sixteenth century the position became much clearer. Turkey and Persia were producing great quantities of carpets, and some of these were being sent to all parts of the known world – to Egypt, North Africa, Spain, Venice of course, and through this great city to the Continent of Europe and England. Eastwards, the craft spread into India, and to Turkestan and China, although the latter may already have developed the art independently. This state of affairs lasted until the latter part of the seventeenth century, when a general decline set in, and it was not until the middle of the nineteenth century that the art was revived, this time due not to court patronage, but to commercial considerations. Today, onee again, production, quality-wise, is at a low ebb, and this time it is possible that the end of the road is in sight. Eventually the hand-knotted product must cease to exist, apart from a few prestige pieces.

The definition of an Oriental carpet or rug is a 'hand knotted product'. Before the hand knotting, however, many processes have to be performed. Wool mainly, and silk rarely, are the chief materials for the pile, whilst either cotton or wool will be needed for the foundation. These raw materials must be sorted, scoured and spun into yarn before the important dyeing procedure. Today, of course, these materials can be purchased already spun, and even dyed to specification, and most of the city-made, and commercially contracted carpets now being produced are made from machine spun yarns. Before this was possible, however, and indeed, in some of the more inaccessible places today, the sheep are locally bred, and every process of manufacture has to be carried out on the spot. All these preparatory processes require great skill, but the weavers are the people who actually produce the end product. However, these weavers are not creative artists in themselves. In the cities and manufacturing centres, even back in the days of court manufacture, they must be guided by designs conceived by artists of the first order and painstakingly drawn upon squared paper – one square for each knot of the carpet. In rural areas and amongst the nomadic peoples other

methods of acquainting the weavers with the design formulae are used, such as drawing in the sand, or having the sequence of colours read or sung out to them. With repetition and long experience, especially in the making of pieces with tribal or other distinctive patterns, the weaver can memorize the sequences and at this stage he or she can work alone without the aids mentioned above.

After the weaving, the carpet has to be sheared and washed, usually in local water or at some central point where the properties of the water are known and recommended. The chemical washing process to which certain modern pieces are subjected is done in Western countries to suit the particular taste of the market.

Basically there are two types of knot used throughout the Orient; the Ghiordes or Turkish knot (which is a full knot); and the Senneh or Persian knot (which is a half knot and can be left- or right-handed).

RIGHT *Detail of a carpet from Heriz, one of the most easily recognized styles of Persian carpets. The completely angular medallion design on a brick red ground colour is quite distinct from the curvilinear patterns typical of Persia as a whole. Most examples date from the last hundred years.*
BELOW *Saruk rug of the nineteenth century, of the style frequently called 'Hamadan', named after a market which is the centre for the products of hundreds of surrounding villages. Saruk rugs are very finely woven and close cropped, with a great clarity of design.*

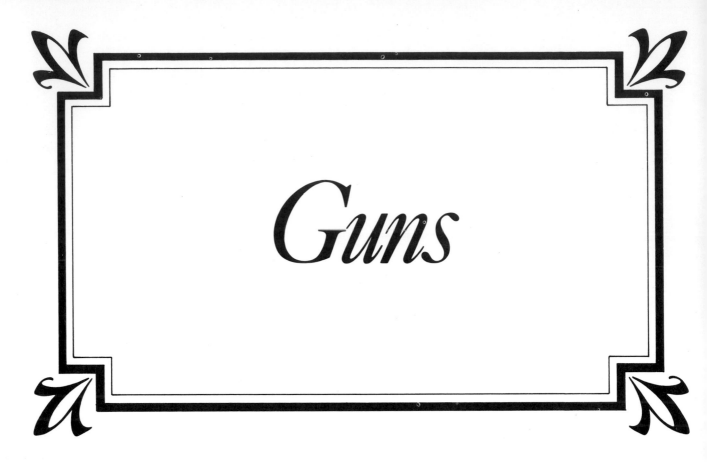

Guns

The idea of actually hurling a projectile by means of gunpowder may not have been tried out until around 1300, and handguns, which were mini-cannons at first, appeared half a century later. A key date was 1326, for in that year the Council of Florence ordered iron bullets and metal barrels to be made for the defence of the city (a document survives to prove it). In that same year Edward III was given a manuscript by his chaplain, Walter de Milemete, which has a coloured picture of a vaselike gun that fired a dart. A knight is shown lighting the charge and the gun appears to be brass.

Early cannon seem to have been simple barrels or tubes, into which were poured the powder, stones or arrows. After the shot was rammed down, the charge was ignited by means of a touch-hole, into which was thrust a red-hot 'firing iron'.

So the 'devil's invention', as some cursed it, inspired a more sinister approach to the business of killing. Although handguns might have a slow rate of fire, they could pierce armour; and even if individually inaccurate, enough of them aimed at a crowd could cause heavy casualties. By the end of the sixteenth century they had made bows obsolete. War as a knightly sport was no longer possible.

Once invented, they were steadily improved. Wooden stocks were introduced in the fourteenth century to help cope with the recoil problem and the heat of the metal; and to speed up the means of ignition the matchlock came into being. What would now be called the action or lockwork appeared with the introduction of the match and the device for holding it.

The match was simply a loosely twisted rope, or hemp wick, which had been soaked in a solution of saltpetre and spirits of wine. When lit, it burned very slowly like a live, glowing coal. Later, the match-holder was attached to the gun. In this form the holder was an S-shaped bar, pivoted in the middle. Beneath it was a pan containing powder which filtered through a touch-hole into the barrel, and when the serpentine (as the match-holder was sometimes called) was lowered, the powder was ignited and the gun discharged.

Gunmakers even then appreciated the value of appearance, and made great efforts to outshine their rival craftsmen. Meanwhile, as it developed, the matchlock underwent various changes in different countries. This resulted in baffling references to hackbuts, hakbuchsen, harquebueses, arquebuses, calivers and petronels. Arque-

A superb pair of French-export flintlock holster pistols. The barrels are chiselled and gilt, and the finely chiselled locks are also gilt. Gold wire has been used as additional decoration for the stocks, and the lavish effect is completed by jewel-encrusted butt caps. They were made by Claude Bizouard of Marseilles in 1857 and presented to Emperor Franz Joseph I.

TOP *The design of this pistol, manufactured by the Belgian company, Fabrique Nationale (F.N.), is a refinement of the famous Colt .45 model made by John Browning in 1911.*

CENTRE *This very ornate south German wheel-lock holster pistol was made for a boy c. 1590; the style of inlay is typical of its period though the piece itself is unusual. The ivory inlay all but disguises the original wood.*

BOTTOM *This is a fine specimen of Colt's .36 calibre six-shot Navy revolver produced at Colt's London Armoury between 1853–6. The pistol is complete in its original box with a cleaning rod, bullet mould, nipple wrench, powder flask and cap box. The small compartment behind the butt contains spare nipples and a spare mainspring.*

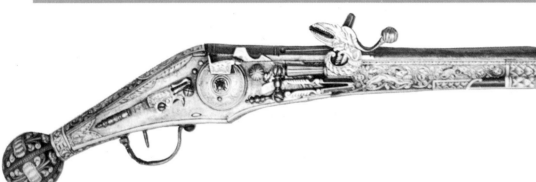

bus meant a weapon fired from the shoulder or chest without a rest.

Though the matchlock survived in varying forms until the late nineteenth century (principally in Japan and India), it was superseded in its own days of glory by a weapon with a far more complicated lock. This was the famous, and still much-admired, wheel-lock, which may be compared with a modern cigarette lighter. A wheel or disc of hardened steel with a serrated rim had a spindle protruding from its centre. This was attached to a small chain, which was connected to a very powerful mainspring. When the wheel was turned, or wound by means of a key or crank, pressure was placed on the mainspring by the chain turning on the spindle. It was kept wound by a simple trigger-like device, which, once released, allowed the wheel to spin with great force. A portion of the wheel protruded into the priming pan, and pressed against it by a spring was a small piece of iron pyrite which gave off sparks. At the same time as the wheel was released by the trigger, another part of the lock pushed aside a cover exposing the pan to the sparks from the iron pyrite. These were directed into the powder and ignited the charge. Although the description sounds complicated, the wheel-lock was simple to use and was developed successfully.

The snaphaunce was a weapon which had a large S-shaped cock containing a flint. The pan containing the priming powder was fitted with a sliding cover activated, when fired, by the cock. The steel against which the flint struck to produce sparks was controlled by a spring, which allowed it to be positioned directly above the pan, or tipped forward out of the way. This latter action produced a safety factor, for unless the steel was in position any accidental tripping of the hammer or cock would not discharge the weapon.

The Dutch were great traders and the 'pecking roosters' reached as far north as Scandinavia (if indeed they did not start there) and as far south as Africa. They were later copied there and, amazingly, 'early' snaphaunces were still being made in Morocco in the 1880s.

One refinement of the snaphaunce was the miquelet, a superior mechanism which was very popular in Spain and Italy. The key factor with this gun was the combination of the steel and the pan. When the cock fell and its flint struck the steel (now L-shaped), which was hinged and held in place by a spring, it knocked it forward, at the same time exposing the pan to the sparks.

A difference between the fashionable locks of the time and the miquelet lock was

A pair of double-barrelled over and under flintlock pistols by John Manton, about 1790. The high quality finish and the elaborate decoration are typical of the best of Manton's work.

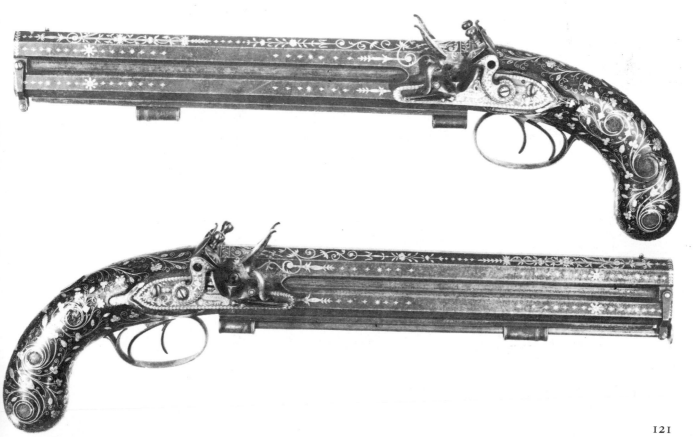

ABOVE *This graceful gun by Stephen Sandwell of London, c. 1765, shows the basic design of the English fowling piece just past the mid-century mark. The long round wrist and shape of the butt are as they had been for the previous fifty years, but the barrel is coming to be held by the flat key or slide, and the surface of the lockplate and cock are usually flat from the end of the 1750s. The Spanish-form or half-octagon barrel is typical.*

BELOW *This silver-mounted sporting gun by Chasteau of Paris, bearing hallmarks for 1772 shows a high quality French gun in the style of the final years of the* ancien régime *before the Revolution brought the Neo-Classical style into a prominence which would last until the early percussion period.*

the presence of the mainspring on the outside of the lock plate – an innovation that proved popular in the Middle East, where, until recently, it was still being used.

The le Bourgeoys or French flintlock, which was widely copied, combined the snaphaunce with the miquelet. From the latter came the combined steel and pan cover (now called the frizzen); from the former was developed the internal mainspring which rested on a tumbler. But le Bourgeoys' most important contribution was the redesigning of the sear, that part of the action which bears upon the hammer notches or 'bents' that provide the half-cock and full-cock positions. In earlier weapons this had moved laterally, but now it had a vertical movement. The improvement in safety and the strength of the lock were quickly realized, and the fame of the invention spread. By the mid-1630s it was known all over Europe.

Each country developed its own version of the flintlock. It altered the whole concept of military hand weapons. With only minor improvements, the flintlock remained the standard ignition for 200 years.

Enthusiasts quickly adapted the new lock to fowling pieces and sporting guns. Pocket

pistols became safer and, with the flintlock, the true duelling pistol appeared. But the main benefit was to the army. By 1700, British military arms were no longer second-class in design or status, and were now standardized and produced in quantity. All over Europe, particularly in France and Germany, guns poured from national armouries at an ever-increasing rate.

The flintlock musket dominated the battlefields of Europe and America from the early 1700s to the 1820s. In France, modifications culminated in the Charleville arms, which were copied by American gunsmiths. Later, the United States Government arms also closely followed French models. But Britain produced the most famous musket of all, the famous Brown Bess.

Its length of service was due to its remarkable durability, simplicity of action and comparative reliability. As a smooth-bore, its accuracy was questionable, but, except in forest and woodland warfare, this did not matter tactically. Several thousand Besses all fired into enemy ranks at 50–200 yards provided real fire power.

Washington's men faced the Brown Bess,

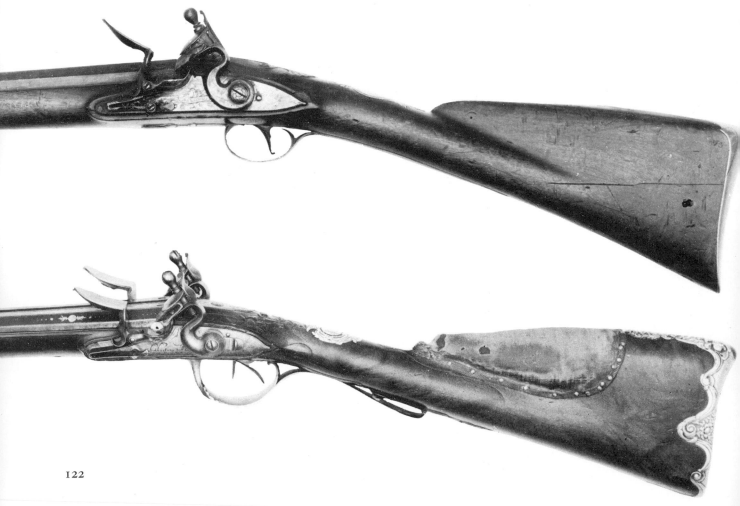

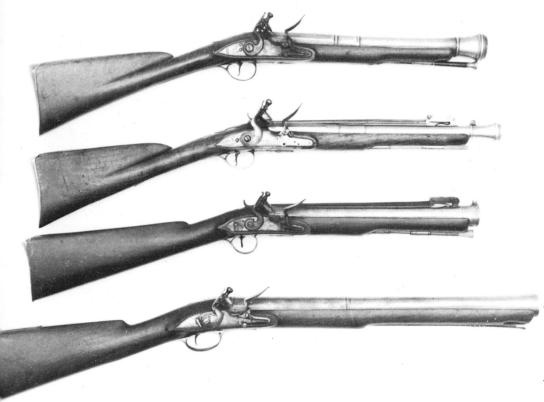

and so did the French in the Peninsula and at Waterloo, where the British squares decimated the French cavalry. Even when it was obsolete, the British sold thousands to Latin America, which meant that in the war against Mexico in 1846–47 the Americans once again found themselves facing the musket of the War of Independence and the War of 1812.

Rivalling the Brown Bess in the War of Independence was the legendary Kentucky rifle, a small-calibred but highly accurate weapon derived from the earlier German Jaeger rifles.

By now the flintlock was a very formidable weapon. Provided it got proper care and attention, that its flints were replaced regularly, and its powder kept dry, it was a good, dependable companion. Refinements were innumerable and by the early nineteenth century it was at its peak as both a smoothbore and a rifled musket. Yet the ultimate in flintlocks proved to be ahead of its time and failed to receive the attention it deserved. This was the Ferguson breechloading rifle.

Experiments continued, and the most practical and efficient invention finally proved to be the percussion cap, paving the way towards the modern metallic cartridge. Credit for this invention is disputed, but many claim that it was an English artist named Joshua Shaw who first introduced a practical cap to replace the previous systems. By mixing the various materials into paste, and placing tiny amounts in minute steel cups or cylinders, it was found that, when placed on the hollow tube or nipple of a firearm, there was enough force to ignite the charge when detonated by the hammer.

Within twenty years, the percussion cap had proved to be the most popular and practical form of ignition. Giant strides were made in its improvement, and the early steel cups or tubes gave way to cups made from very thin sheets of copper. The fulminate of mercury or potassium chlorate, covered by a sheet of tinfoil and sealed with shellac, became the standard ingredient. The system was now much simpler.

At the breech of the gun was screwed the tube or nipple, through the centre of which was drilled a hole leading directly to the powder charge. The cap was placed over the face of the nipple and, when struck by the hammer, it exploded, the flame setting off the charge. Whereas the flintlock had been subject to misfires from poor flints or from damp, the percussion lock proved its reliability under most conditions, and flintlock weapons very gradually disappeared from use altogether.

As with most forms of firearms, it was the sportsmen who first popularized the percussion lock, and the military who followed suit. On the Continent, the percussion lock was quickly adopted by various armies, but Britain was curiously slow at accepting the new system. Nevertheless, the civilian arms trade was soon booming.

Among the most significant trends stemming from the percussion lock was a massive increase in the production of single- and multi-shot pistols. Whereas the flintlock pistol had mainly been designed to be carried in saddle holsters (so that only in the early years of the nineteenth century had pocket or coat pistols been made in any great number) the invention of the percussion lock inspired the more general use of smaller arms. This was particularly true in the United States where a pistol was as much a part of a man's dress as his boots.

Perhaps the most famous of all pocket pistols were those made by the Philadelphia gunsmith, Henry Deringer Jr. For years he had been an arms contractor for the U.S. Government, making both military and Indian guns, but after 1825, when he switched to the percussion lock, he concentrated on single-shot pistols. His early arms were long-barrelled weapons, best suited to the belt, but when customers began asking him to cut down the length of the barrels, he experimented with weapons which, although much smaller than his standard arms, retained the large calibres. Tests proved that, despite their size, they were easily handled, and deadly accurate at short ranges.

The response was immediate and Deringer's name became a household word. Scores of his new pocket pistols were ordered and the design became so popular that it was widely copied. Measuring less than 6 inches in length, and with calibres from .36 to .45 (.41 being the most favoured), the Deringer, in its way, became as famous as Colt's revolver.

It was the American Samuel Colt who finally produced the first practical and reliable revolver. In 1835, he patented the design in England, and a year later in the U.S.A. The system was amazingly simple, yet ingenious. The cylinder or breech revolved on an axis, or spindle attached to the barrel, which in turn was held on by a wedge. Each time the hammer was pulled back, a hand or pawl attached to it turned the cylinder, so that a chamber lined up with the bore.

The earliest Colt's revolvers were five-shooters. They were made at an armoury at

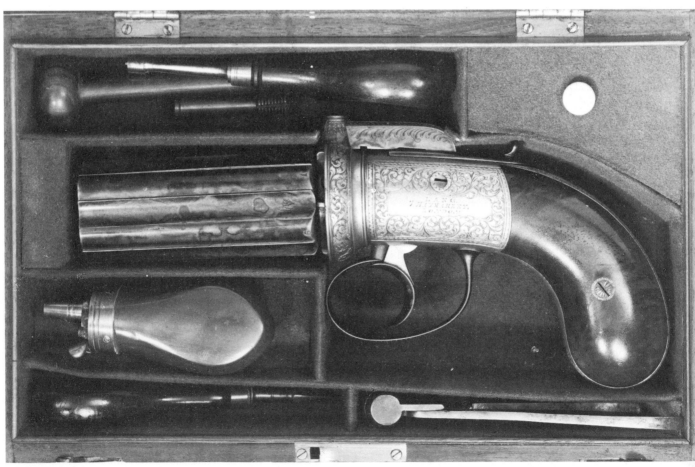

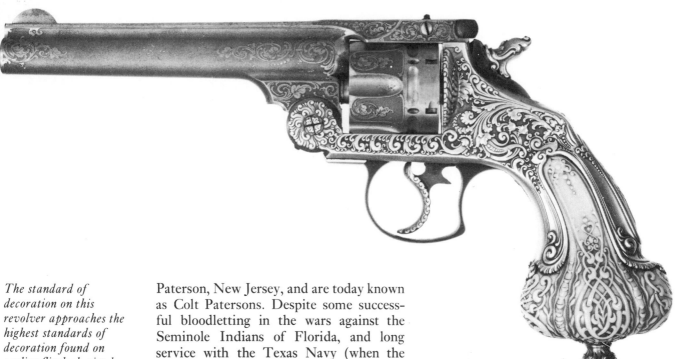

The standard of decoration on this revolver approaches the highest standards of decoration found on earlier flintlock pistols.

Paterson, New Jersey, and are today known as Colt Patersons. Despite some successful bloodletting in the wars against the Seminole Indians of Florida, and long service with the Texas Navy (when the state was independent) and the Texas Rangers, by the early 1840s the Paterson venture was over. But in 1846, at the insistence of Captain Samuel Walker, a former Texas Ranger, and now a captain in the U.S. Regiment of Mounted Rifles, the U.S. Government ordered 1,000 revolvers from Colt for use in its war of expansion against Mexico. In view of Walker's criticism of the Paterson revolver, Colt redesigned it. In place of the folding trigger previously used, he fitted a standard trigger guard and simplified the action. It is worth noting that this single-action mechanism (in which the hammer had to be thumb-cocked for each shot) is still employed today in Colt's Single Action Army, or Peacemaker, revolvers.

The success of the new revolver, known to history as the Colt-Walker Dragoon, quickly led to new orders, and Colt built a factory in his home town of Hartford, Connecticut. During the Crimean War, he set up another factory in London where he produced thousands of his Navy model revolvers which he sold to the British Government.

Successors to the Walker revolver included a modified version, the 1848 Dragoon, followed by the 1848 and 1849 pocket pistols, the 1851 and 1861 Navy revolvers and the 1860 Army revolver. There was a steady demand for these and similar weapons, for this was an age in which a man without a pistol was not considered properly dressed. Consequently Sam Colt reigned supreme in his field until

he died in 1862. The most successful pistol produced during his lifetime was the 1851 Navy revolver. Wild Bill Hickok, perhaps the only gunfighter whose life matched his legend, carried a pair of these revolvers through most of his career, wearing them butt forward in belt or holsters for the reverse draw, so popular on the Plains.

Colt had many rivals. On the Continent, the Frenchman, Casimir Lefaucheux had pioneered the famous pinfire system in the early 1850s and this was quickly adopted by the French Government. The cartridge had a metal base, a paper or metal tube containing a powder charge, and a conical bullet. Seated in the base of the cartridge was a percussion pellet attached to a small pin, which protruded from the side of the case. When struck by the hammer, this pin detonated the charge. Examples of the pinfire system were shown at the Great Exhibition in 1851, but the pinfire was not popular in Britain.

Colt's American rivals included Remington (who also pioneered the typewriter and the sewing machine in the 1870s) and, later, Smith and Wesson. This team obtained the exclusive rights to produce bored-through cylinders to take metallic ammunition under a patent granted to Rollin White in 1855. As early as 1857, Smith and Wesson were producing small-calibred rimfire revolvers. The odd situation whereby they alone had the right to produce commercial breechloading metallic cartridge revolvers in the U.S.A. lasted until the patent expired in 1869.

In Europe, where no such restrictions existed, various forms of fixed ammunition were being used in the early 1860s and within a few years the percussion revolver had largely been replaced. Yet until the late 1870s, some British Army officers were still using percussion pistols because of the unreliable state of metallic ammunition at that time.

The most famous Colt revolver was the Single Action Army model of 1873, known as the Peacemaker or the Frontier. In the .45-calibre version it remained the standard sidearm of the U.S. Cavalry until 1890. Among its principal competitors were the Smith and Wesson 'American' and 'Russian' models (the latter developed for Czarist Russia), their Schofield revolver, and Remington's new Model Army revolver of 1875.

Whether revolvers were made in Britain, Europe, the U.S.A., Japan or Russia, their use was always dictated by necessity and practicability. In Britain the Army had experimented with Colt's revolvers as a means of rearming infantry as early as 1852; and in 1854 it tested the Navy Dragoon models at distances of over 400 yards, with good results. But it was soon realized that few soldiers could be expected to be as accurate as experts. So the revolver was reduced in status to a secondary weapon, and was chiefly used by officers and mounted troops.

The United States, by tradition, retained the revolver as an indispensable personal asset, and even today it has a place in military thinking. But its greatest fame was on the Frontier, where it played a major role in formulating the myth of the Wild West.

The simplicity and reliability of the revolver had led to its being retained as the principal weapon of many of the world's police forces.

From the time of the first matchlocks, weapons had been made for hunting. Long-barrelled fowling pieces were very popular, and whereas most hunters restricted their activities to open spaces and woodlands, many were prosecuted for using firearms too close to towns and villages. By the seventeenth century, birding, as it was called, knew no social barriers, and even poorer people engaged in it.

Each new generation introduced new ideas and inventions. The popularity of hunting, and its patronage by Louis XIII of France and other monarchs, did much to promote increased interest in shooting, and by the eighteenth century the flintlock fowling piece had become an object of beauty and fine balance which earned it a place in the forefront of sporting weapons well into the nineteenth century. Once the percussion lock became generally accepted, so too did new sporting guns which made use of it, and a new word appeared in the English language – the shotgun.

Today, nearly all long guns, except shotguns, are rifled, i.e. spiral-grooved, but the terminology has only been in use for less than 200 years. Before the mid-eighteenth century most shoulder arms were smoothbore and were generally called muskets or 'musquets'. But by the early years of the nineteenth century things were changing fast. In place of the smoothbore arms, an increasing number of guns were made with spiral grooves running from the breech to the muzzle.

Early German immigrants to what was later Pennsylvania brought with them the Jaeger rifle, and from this was developed the so-called Kentucky rifle of the Revolutionary War. Its original home is thought to have been in Lancaster County, Pennsylvania, where a number of German gunsmiths were known to have settled. Whereas the Jaeger had been primarily a sporting weapon, the new rifle was designed to meet the needs of frontiersman and hunter alike. Most were produced in small calibres from .30 to .45, but some were made with bores as high as .80. The weight was considerably reduced, and the streamlined appearance made it very distinctive.

The Americans were not alone in developing new ideas. A breechloading rifled musket was the invention of a Scotsman from Aberdeenshire, Captain Patrick Ferguson. His design owed something to the earlier work of the Frenchman, Isaac de la Chaumette, but his improvements made the weapon far more practical. A threaded plug attached to the trigger guard was turned down, exposing the breech. Into this were poured powder and ball, and the trigger guard was turned up and locked into position. Then the gun was primed and fired in the normal way.

Ferguson's rifle had many successors. In the United States, John Hall was one of several who produced a breechloader; and

TOP *This Swiss rifle is by B. von Reinach of Basle, and is dated 1619. The lockplate is of wheel-lock pattern and it appears that the rifle has been converted back to the matchlock system. It is fitted with a hair trigger. The .67 calibre barrel is 50 in. in length.*

CENTRE *Browning over and under shotgun 'Grand Luxe' Type D4G with special engraving of the highest quality by Vrancken.*

BOTTOM *The snaphaunce lock early developed into several regional variations across the continent of Europe, this example being a central Italian version of about 1750. The principal feature which distinguishes it from the true flintlock is the separation into two parts of the steel and the pan cover. Most sporting snaphaunces have pan covers automatically removed by the action of the tumble or other internal arrangements.*

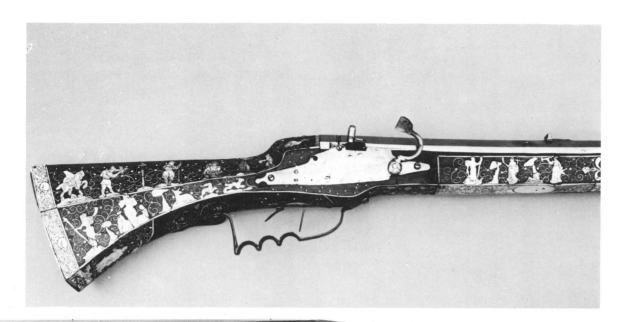

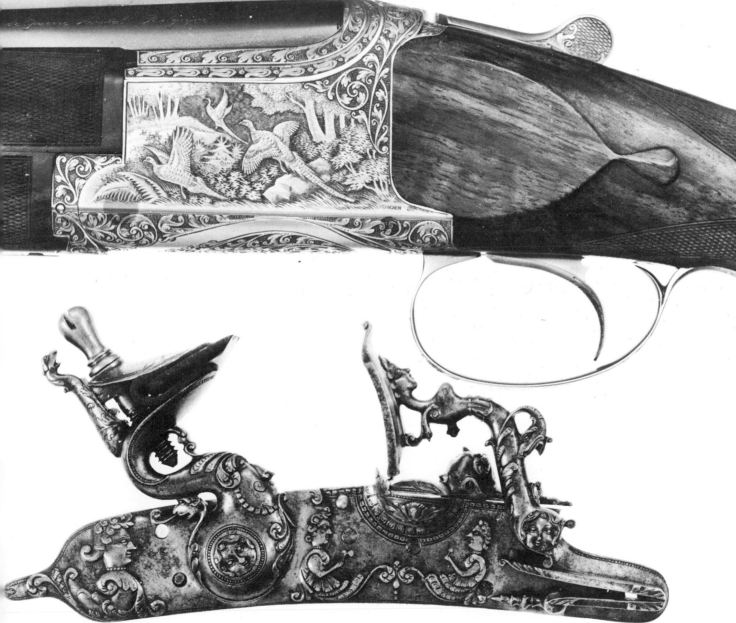

in Switzerland, Samuel Johannes Pauly also invented one, his innovation being ammunition in the form of an expanding cartridge case, which sealed off the escape of flame and gases. Pauly was followed by his Prussian protégé, Johann von Dreyse, whose experiments at a percussion-cap factory, of which he was part-owner, led to two successes – the famous needle gun in the 1820s and a breechloader in 1837. The Dreyse system was a lead bullet hollowed out to take a primer in its base. This was exploded by a long needlelike firing pin, which passed right through the powder charge and struck the primer.

Change was in the air. The rimfire cartridge proved reliable and was used by many arms-makers, particularly in the American Civil War. This was a copper or brass case

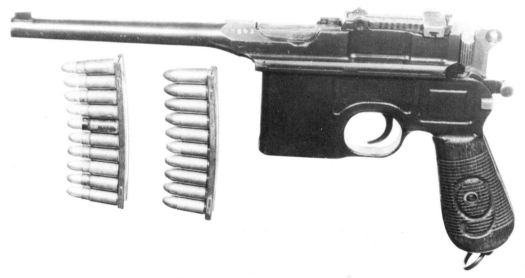

containing bullet and powder, the base of which was covered with a fulminate. Modern .22 ammunition is identical to that of the 1860s. Although percussion rifles, muskets and revolvers were the main weapons of the Civil War, the breech-loading arms of the Sharps, the Spencer (a seven-shot weapon) and others were joined by the new Henry rifle, a sixteen-shot rimfire that was replaced in 1866 by the renowned Winchester.

The first Winchester was a great success on the Plains, and in 1873 came perhaps the most famous rifle of them all, the Winchester '73, often called 'The Gun that Won the West'. It does not deserve all the credit, but its rapid fire was certainly an important factor. On that hot June day in 1876 when General Custer and his entire command were wiped out at the Little Big Horn, a few Winchester '73s might have prolonged

the battle, though it would not have affected the result. As it was, too many of the men fought with defective Springfield carbines which jammed, became overheated and so failed to work.

As the guns improved, so did the ammunition. Rimfire gave way to centre-fire, still in use today. The case is made of a drawn brass tube, at the bottom of which is placed the cap or primer. By the 1880s, having progressed from earlier forms made of paper and skin (animal entrails), the cartridge, now made of metal, had reached perfection. In fact today's cartridges are almost unchanged.

Since the early days of guns, there had been many attempts at producing repeating weapons. When Hiram Maxim discovered that the recoil forces could be used to

recock a firearm, the first automatic weapons were produced.

Progress, after Maxim's discovery, was rapid. John M. Browning produced a fully automatic machine gun for Colt's; the British produced the Vickers and Lewis guns, while on the Continent great strides were being made by a number of companies. By World War I, the machine gun was an integral part of most armies, though the more conservative generals underrated it. The slaughter of the British Army by the Germans on 1 July 1916, the first day of the Battle of the Somme, clinched the matter.

In addition to machine guns, smaller automatic weapons were developed. France, Germany and America all worked on the problem. From Germany came two of the most successful, the Mauser (1898) and the Luger (1900).

Oriental Arts

The past 80 to 100 years have witnessed an enormous increase in our interest in the history of the Far East. Before about 1900 we had little more than legend; since then, and beginning with railway construction, the greed of the tomb robber and the carefully controlled spade of the archaeologist have unearthed some remarkable objects wholly beyond the imagination of the early nineteenth century, particularly bronzes. The astonishing thing about these bronzes, which go back to the second millennium BC, is that, though austere, brutal and dignified, they are also highly sophisticated and compel the conclusion that even the earliest among them represents, not the start of a new technique, but one which must surely have had its origin in the more distant past, for it is difficult to believe that such powerful designs could have sprung up suddenly.

Legend has it that it was the Emperor Yü, fifth in descent from the Yellow Emperor (mid-third millennium BC) who first had bronze vessels cast. There may well be some truth in the tradition that after Yü had dealt successfully with a great flood he had nine bronze cauldrons cast, one each for his nine provinces. These became imperial symbols, and were handed down from emperor to emperor and were still in

existence in the sixth century BC in the lifetime of Confucius. The last of the Chou Dynasty emperors had them thrown into the river to prevent them falling into the hands of his enemies.

Fact and folklore are inextricably mingled, but archaeology has tended to confirm the antiquity of these early bronzes. As yet, though, none have been found which can be dated definitely earlier than the Shang-Yin Dynasty (1525–1028 BC). It seems more than likely that as floods in the Yellow River area were frequent throughout recorded history there must be many bronzes and other objects still lying buried deep in the earth.

The bronzes which have been found are mostly household treasures used both for ritual purposes and for ordinary domestic use – tripods, ewers, storage vessels and containers for grain. A family's importance was measured to some extent by the number of its bronzes; some of them were inlaid with gold or silver and those from the late Chou period include a great variety of implements and fittings – pole finials, axes, swords with grips inlaid with turquoise, animal figures, and also personal things such as combs, pins, pendants and mirrors. Many of the ritual bronzes carry inscrip-

Archaic bronze covered wine vessel, or Yu, Western Chou dynasty, late eleventh century BC. Ritual vessels of this type are the most important surviving indications of the quality of Chinese art and design at this early period. The colours of the vessel have occurred naturally during centuries of burial.

tions bearing witness to the prestige of the family within their social group.

On the whole the late Chou pieces lack the incisive vigour of their predecessors and with the Han Dynasty (206 BC–AD 220), the style for bronzes as for other things became simpler and inlays of gold and silver, turquoise and malachite more frequent. There were, though, fine things produced during the succeeding centuries, notably small human and animal figures and – thanks to the introduction of Buddhism – numerous gilt-bronze images of Buddha himself and his followers.

The honour paid to jade by the Chinese throughout their history is unique in the world – no other people has seen in it the epitome of all virtue. Men, said Confucius, have found it smooth and shining like benevolence; fine, compact and strong like intelligence; its edges, like justice, look sharp but do not cut; when struck it gives forth a clear musical note; like truth, it does not conceal flaws and so adds to its beauty; it is bright as heaven and yet its substance, contained in hills and streams, is like earth. Even the Chinese word for it, Yü, signifies also the five cardinal virtues: charity, modesty, courage, justice and wisdom.

Jade is of course a hardstone. Geology recognizes two sorts – nephrite and jadeite. It was found in the river beds in the form of pebbles and then, as supplies became scarce, began to be imported first from Turkestan and then, during the thirteenth century, from Burma. It is carved by lapidaries by means of a treadle device, the jade piece held against the tubular drill and rotated and moved about as required.

In the West the word jade has long been used to describe a colour, an olive green. But the mineral itself can be any colour from yellow to black with a particular off-white a great favourite – a cream colour the Chinese described not very poetically as mutton fat. The jade carvers were – and indeed are – often brilliant in making use of faults in their pebble as they work at it. Stories of their ingenuity are endless.

The earliest jades recorded were found on various Neolithic sites (3000–2500 BC). In later centuries – jades for instance found in Shang-Yin Dynasty tombs – there are various pendants and plaques in silhouette of animals and birds (presumably secular ornaments) and various very highly stylized ritual objects. Decoration on all these early jades is very slight. The material

RIGHT *Chinese* blanc de chine *figure of the goddess Kuan-yin, an example of the pure white porcelain made in the eighteenth century in the province of Fukien.*

LEFT *Chinese figure of a cat, K'ang Hsi period, 1662–1722, decorated with mottled glazes in the Tang style. There is a legend that at Buddha's funeral, while all the other animals stood round weeping, the cat turned away to chase a rat. The cat was punished by having its gaze fixed for ever on the Golden Goblet of the Buddha, hence the cross-eyed look of this figure.*

was always regarded as having magical properties in itself.

Gradually the awe with which the stone had been regarded down to nearly the beginning of our era evaporated and the carvers began to come into their own. Jade was still respected as noble and precious but it was valued also as a vehicle for fine and ingenious decoration. Little three-dimensional jade charms were much in demand, both in animal and human forms; jade beads and bracelets, jade sword hilts, buckles, hair ornaments, necklaces and pendants have all been found in Han Dynasty tombs. A few centuries later in the T'ang Dynasty the most famous of beauties Yang Kuei-fei, celebrated in song and story, danced to the sound of jade flutes and is said to have slept in a jade bed.

Moving on through yet more centuries people of standing in the Sung Dynasty (AD 960–1279) – an age of extraordinary refinement in all the arts from painting to ceramics – were interested mostly in white and green jades, it is said because these colours were close to the beautiful near-white and celadon ceramics of the period. In fact it was the other way about – they

133

admired the ceramics because they come close to the colours of so much of the jades. This was also a time when artists looked back to the glories of the past, and so many jades were carved in the form of the ancient bronzes.

Until this time the abrasive used was sand but there is a record of a new type being produced at the time of the Mongol invasion described as black sand which is thought to mean the far more efficient carborundum. If that is so, it helps perhaps to account for the enormous output of carved jade throughout the succeeding centuries. Certainly from the beginning of the Ming Dynasty (AD 1368–1664) onwards the variety of jade carvings passes belief.

In addition to useful, if luxurious objects,

there were jades made according to the ancient manner for religious ceremonies, particularly those for the emperor at the regular sacrifices, and also the carefully modulated jade chimes for the orchestras which performed ritual music at the Altar of Heaven and the Temple of Confucius. Yet among all this enormous output most westerners find the small charms – usually beasts or birds or flowers – the most endearing. These were made to be carried on the person and fondled in the hand from time to time. Their form is usually dictated by their markings, each is therefore unique and made to be turned about and seen from every angle.

As with bronzes and jades one has to travel far back in time to find the origins of Chinese ceramics. The archaeologist has revealed that the industry, in spite of disasters, had experienced a continual development during a period of at least 4,000 years.

It seems astonishing that within living

FAR LEFT *Chinese lacquer tray, inlaid with mother of pearl, Ming Dynasty, 1368–1644.*

ABOVE *Japanese wood block print of girls paddling in a river, from the Furyu Mu-Tamagawa by Utamaro, published in about 1790. Japanese prints of this type greatly influenced European art and design during the latter part of the nineteenth century.*

BELOW *Large plate decorated in underglaze blue with a scene of birds in a garden, the rim with moulded peony flowers, Yuan dynasty, about AD 1350. This style of Chinese decoration greatly influenced the design of European porcelain in the eighteenth century.*

*Japanese Eine vase,
typical of the export
wares produced during the
nineteenth century by the
Japanese Satsuma
province, decorated with
elaborate gilding and
raised enamels.*

memory only a very few Westerners had any inkling of the achievements of anonymous Chinese potters before, say, about the year 1500. We knew next to nothing about the refinements of the Sung Dynasty masters, even less about the achievements of their predecessors, and disbelieved any story which hinted at even earlier triumphs.

The difficulty in writing about Chinese pots within the limits of this book arises from their bewildering variety, but a few of the outstanding types may be indicated. By the middle of the Han Dynasty, the glazing of pottery – a lead glaze – had become fairly common. When it was not enamelled the pot would perhaps be covered with white clay and painted, usually red or black. A fairly familiar type found in Han tombs is a dignified jar modelled on contemporaty bronze forms.

With T'ang Dynasty wares, a vast and dazzling number of tomb figures have been unearthed: horses, servants, musicians, camels all placed in the tomb with the dead grandee to serve him in the land of shadows. They are lively and colourful so that we are liable to forget the less dramatic domestic wares – the vases, dishes and so forth which can be very fine and are naturally rare. It is now that we first hear of porcelain – true porcelain by which in the West is meant a substance which, though made of clay, is translucent. Fragments of such porcelain have been found as far afield as Samarra on the Tigris, a city founded in 836 and abandoned in 883 – proof positive that by the ninth century the Chinese could make a substance which was vitrified, resonant, white and translucent. It was a great achievement, particularly because the aim of these early potters was to produce something resembling jade.

The Sung Dynasty which followed marks for some the highest point Chinese potters ever reached. The objects are very quiet, their effect depending upon beauty of form and delicacy of glaze; what decoration there is, was engraved or impressed on the clay before glazing and there was only one firing. Porcelain now became recognized, not as just a substitute for bronze or jade, but as an art in its own right. The best known of the Sung wares are the magnificent dishes, olive-green in colour, which were exported in quantity – heavy and a trifle coarse, but noble objects none the less, and popular in the Middle East because it was put about that poisoned food changed colour in them, a useful selling point in difficult times. Apart from the celadons, several other wares have attracted the admiration of East and West alike. The rarest of them, Ju ware, was made for imperial use during a few brief years before the Tartar invasion.

White in China was always the colour of mourning, so when the court or a great household suffered the loss of its head or someone near to him, all dishes, etc. had to be white: hence Ting ware, made at Ting Chou during the T'ang Dynasty and brought to perfection under the Sung emperors. Next there is Ying Ch'ing ware (shadowy blue), the lustrous dark brown or black bowls with brown streaks or splashes or silvery oil spots, and a range of Chün wares – flowerpots, bulb bowls and wine pots – the material heavy, the colours ranging from a light blue or lavender to crimson and purple in apparently haphazard patches. Finally there is a less exalted kind, made for ordinary use: Tz'u Chou ware, a stoneware covered with a white slip, glazed and with fine freehand drawing above that in brown or black, occasionally painting in red and green. Sometimes the white slip was scratched away round the decoration.

The next step was painting in blue under the glaze and it was this technique which was the chief glory of the early years of the Ming Dynasty. Few objects in the world of porcelain can be finer than a blue and white dish of the late fourteenth or early fifteenth centuries; particularly those which can be assigned to the reign of the Emperor Hsüan Tê (1426–35), for by then the Chinese were importing a very choice cobalt from the Near East known as Mohammedan blue, which was combined with the darker native product. At the same time experiments were undertaken with other colours, especially red, derived from copper. In all these early wares the drawing is wonderfully bold and free.

By the reign of Ch'êng Hua (1465–87) eggshell-thin porcelain was being produced, as notable for the quality of its material as for the delicacy of its painting – a type extensively and beautifully copied during the eighteenth century. In addition to all this, monochromes were much in demand: yellow (for imperial use), turquoise blue, dark blue, green, brown, red and black, and, not least among many marvels, the pure ivory pieces from Fukien made in Ming times certainly; as soon as

they reached Europe the French considered them to epitomize the skills of the whole industry and called them *blanc de Chine*, by which name they have been known ever since.

After this one might imagine no further triumphs were possible or desirable. There were in fact several: some new monochrome glaze developed in the reign of K'ang Hsi (1662–1722), the various styles we know as *famille noire* and *famille jaune*, and *famille verte*, much blue and white. The eighteenth century witnessed the wide range of *famille rose* colourings, yet more variations of monochrome glazes, and (during the brief reign of Yung Chêng, 1723–36) some superb dishes and other vessels painted with flowers and figures set off with wonderful subtlety by large areas of empty space. Many of these pieces were brought

Eighteenth-century lacquered cabinet of the type exported to the West by the East India Companies. Cabinets of this type were made in both China and Japan and decorated in gold on a black or coloured ground. This example stands on the floor, but it was customary in Europe from the second half of the seventeenth century to mount such cabinets on stands which often bore no stylistic relationship to the subtle oriental workmanship.

to Europe in the ships of the East India Company, as part of the enormous Chinese and Japanese export trades of the eighteenth century.

Lacquer is unique to the Far East. It is a white resinous sap derived from the lactree (*Rhus vernicifera*). When exposed to the light it turns black and takes any colour. By about 1000 BC the Chinese were aware of its remarkable properties: it polished beautifully, was an excellent preservative for wood, and was impervious to damp. It was always regarded as something of a luxury because of the infinite time and patience and exceptional skill required to produce any lacquer piece of quality.

There were two kinds of lacquer work, painted and carved. In the first method wood would be planed down paper thin and over this layer upon layer of the coloured lacquer would be painted. Each layer had to dry thoroughly before the next could be applied and so, as in the finest pieces, as many as twenty or thirty layers might be required, it is easy to see how expensive the final result could be. The second method

was even more laborious and time consuming – indeed in some cases ten years was regarded as not at all exceptional. The lacquer had to be built up layer upon layer in such a manner that there could well be three layers each perhaps one tenth of an inch in depth in different colours. When that was thoroughly dry the task of the carver was to cut through the surface in such a way that he produced a design which made use of all three colours – a work demanding an extreme nicety of judgment, not to mention a steady hand and a monumental concentration. The slightest slip could ruin many months of work.

Apart from the evidence provided by the excavation of Chou and Han Dynasty tombs there are precious survivals preserved in Japan, namely T'ang Dynasty lacquered pieces deposited in the Imperial Treasure House at Nara by the widow of a Japanese emperor who died in AD 756. Most of the T'ang and Sung lacquer is decorated simply with floral designs on a dark ground. A certain number of pieces have survived with inlay of mother-of-pearl and touches

ABOVE RIGHT *Chinese export porcelain vase of the eighteenth century, decorated in the* famille rose *style. The vase is supported by two figures of Dutchmen, which reflects the domination of the Dutch East India Company in the Far East trade.*

BELOW RIGHT *Ivory netsuke carved as a wild boar lying among leaves by Totamada, an eighteenth-century artist of the Kioto School.*

BELOW *Chinese model of a horse, carved from grey jade, Ming Dynasty. This shows how well the jade carver could exploit the natural markings of the stone.*

of gold and silver – a technique which in the West is known as *lac burgauté* and which the Chinese called 'misty brocade'.

The great age for lacquer work is generally considered that under the Ming Emperors, partly because of the vigour of the designs and the fact – which does not seem to be explained – that Ming cinnabar is darker than that of the eighteenth century.

As time passed and commerce, particularly the export trade, demanded speed, quality was bound to suffer, but even pieces which would not satisfy the high standards of the Chinese connoisseur can still be charming. It is perhaps worth reminding ourselves of the enthusiasm with which lacquer was greeted in Europe. Madame de Pompadour made a collection which is now in the Louvre in Paris, and before that in 1688 in a practical How To Do It book Messrs Stalker & Parker had enthusiastically encouraged the English to 'japan' furniture. Unfortunately we cannot grow the lactree here and so had to make do with copal varnish, which is quite different.

The arts of Japan are perhaps less well known than those of China, mainly because few examples were seen in Europe until the nineteenth century. Japanese ceramics, which range from the low-fired *raku* earthenwares to the fine porcelains of Arita and Nankin, and the richly ornamented nineteenth century wares of Satsuma and 'Old Imari', have also been influential in Europe, particularly among the studio potters of the last hundred years. In Japan the carving of ivory has in some ways been the equivalent of jade carving in China. *Netsuke* are a good example of the carver's skill. These minute, highly detailed, and now highly prized objects were originally made as toggles, to hold the rope worn round the waist. They occur in a great variety of styles and forms, and were frequently used as a display of technical virtuosity on the part of the carver. Like jade, the carver could often see the form of his design latent in the ivory. Animal forms are particularly attractive.

The Japanese were also masters of lacquer, although their work was often on a more miniature scale. Typical are *inro*, richly decorated collections of vessels to hold ink or paint which hung at the end of two cards attached to the *netsuke*. These were later often used for medicines, a purse, tinder box, a drinking gourd or a tobacco-pouch.

Perhaps Japan's greatest contribution to European art is the print. The first examples were seen in Europe in the nineteenth century, and had an immediate impact on the modern painters of the day; the vibrant and revolutionary styles of the Impressionists owed much to the Japanese print. The great variety of style and technique seen in Japanese prints has made them popular among collectors both rich and poor.

OPPOSITE *Inro, or artist's box made by Shibata Zeshin, nineteenth century, with a decoration of plants and flowers in gold, silver and grey lacquer on a brown wood-grain lacquer ground.*

THIS PAGE *Rectangular rosewood table on square legs, typical of Chinese eighteenth-century furniture. The carved fretwork decoration greatly influenced English furniture designers such as Chippendale.*

Art Nouveau

Think of a sensuous line; of a flowing line; a line which bends and turns back on itself. Think too, of controlled lines: lines which begin parallel but then converge and eventually contradict each other. Think of the resulting stress. As the English artist, Walter Crane, one of the earliest exponents of the New Art said in 1889: 'Line is all-important. Let the designer, therefore, in the adaptation of his art, lean upon the staff of line – line determinative, line emphatic, line delicate, line expressive, line controlling and uniting.'

Then think of all this expressed in architecture, rooms, furniture, ceramics, glass, jewelry, the printed page, posters, coffee pots, lamps and cutlery and you will have some idea what Art Nouveau is all about.

But no period of art arrives complete and ready-made. There are always influences working, often centuries back. One can trace Art Nouveau ideas in Celtic, Gothic, Rococo and Japanese art. The Industrial Revolution upset the balance of a natural progression from one art period to another by making reproduction of past forms all too easy. Rumblings of discontent can be traced to writers in the late eighteenth century when the machine began to take over, but it was left to the 1851 Exhibition at the Crystal Palace in London to set off the first blast of real reaction.

Here we discover a paradox. The Crystal Palace was in itself a revolutionary step. Iron and glass were used to create a simple, startling, functional statement. It looked like a fairy bubble; but it was a bubble which worked. Ironically the contents which it housed, gathered from all over the world, did not measure up to their packing. All the products so proudly displayed were then considered to be in the best 'good taste'. It was left to William Morris, an inspired, far-seeing and socialist artist, to call it 'tons upon tons of unutterable rubbish'.

Morris is the touchstone for the Art Nouveau movement. In 1861, he, in collaboration with others, set up the Arts and Crafts Movement. Everything was to be handmade. Furniture, tapestries, wallpapers, fabrics, pottery: all had to be objects of beauty *and* use. The joy of the craftsman in his work would ensure that the work itself was beautiful. And this beauty would immediately be accepted and appreciated by the buyer. Morris wanted art for everyone, just as he wanted education and freedom for everyone.

But he did not realize that handmade

Silver gilt salt cellar designed by C. R. Ashbee, and made by the Guild of Handicrafts at Chipping Camden, 1900. The mixture of medieval and contemporary styles is typical of the English Art Nouveau movement.

products would be far too expensive for the masses, who, under increasing industrialization, were becoming even poorer. He did not appreciate that Victorian society was in no way comparable to the medieval one. Sincere as he was, his vision was doomed to failure from the beginning.

He did, however, set the ball rolling. Without his vision, few of the succeeding Arts and Crafts Societies, the shops, the Arts Centres, the schools, the exhibitions, the magazines and journals, would have happened. One of his most imaginative disciples was Arthur H. Mackmurdo, who founded the Century Guild in 1881. Like Morris, he was typical of the 'new' artist, in that he designed *all* forms of domestic articles. This diversification was to be the outstanding hallmark of succeeding Art Nouveau artists. There were few who were not able to design cutlery with the same skill that they put into a building, a piece of furniture or a painting.

Other groups soon followed. Walter Crane, book-designer and illustrator, founded the Art Workers' Guild in 1884. The Arts and Crafts Exhibition Society and the Guild of Handicrafts, the latter inaugurated by C. R. Ashbee, started in 1899.

In 1862 an exhibition of Japanese goods was held in Paris. The whole stand was subsequently bought by an English firm, who put Arthur Lazenby Liberty in charge of their new Oriental department in London. When the firm closed, in 1874, Mr Liberty bought its stock and opened his own shop in Regent Street. Thus the famous firm was born, and thus, due to the fact that Liberty and Co. patronized and encouraged Art Nouveau artists, the name *Stile Liberty* was given to the movement at one of its stages.

The initial impetus therefore, was English, and its earliest exponent in England was Mackmurdo. In architecture and furniture he used a narrow vertical line which was to influence such architects as Voysey and Mackintosh. His stylization took natural forms and translated them into abstraction, without losing the original inspiration.

C. R. Ashbee, architect and silversmith, produced the typical English solution to life and art: that of compromise. Closely allied to the Arts and Crafts movement he was also an important influence on the early Art Nouveau movement.

Charles Annesley Voysey was another English artist at whom the rather unflatter-

BELOW *Satinwood cabinet with inset painted panels, designed by E. W. Godwin, about 1877. In this piece, Godwin mixes Japonisme with romantic medievalism.*

ing title of 'compromiser' can be levied. Influenced by Japanese art, he excelled in domestic architecture and his houses were particularly successful in their precise proportions, subtle asymmetry and understated ornament.

Like prophets, many of these English artists and architects received more recognition abroad than in their own country. Such a one was Hugh Ballie Scott, furniture designer and architect who used Art Nouveau elements as design on flat surfaces rather than on whole pieces.

Aubrey Beardsley, one of the most famous of English artists has, through recent popularization, become synonymous

with Art Nouveau. As with Toulouse-Lautrec, Beardsley was a genius in his own right and used Art Nouveau to suit his purpose. His well-known illustrations for Oscar Wilde's *Salome* with their Japanese feeling, stylized women, roses and peacocks are a case in point.

Although it was principally English reaction to the accepted mode, the influence of the Arts and Crafts Movement and like guilds, which persuaded Continental artists also to rebel, little of any importance was later produced in England, although it was kept alive by *The Studio* journal and by Liberty in his shop in Regent Street.

English designers and artists exhibited their new-found freedom at Brussels in the late 1880s and also in 1892: it was in this year that one of the brightest stars of the Movement, the Belgian architect Victor Horta (1861–1947), began to plan the first important Continental house to be built in Art Nouveau style. This was the Maison Tassel in Brussels. Completed in 1893, it is a watershed of Art Nouveau design, combining as it does both two- and three-dimensional architectural features and decoration. He used wrought-iron in a new way: particularly in the staircase for this house, a poem of fairy-like tendrils, plant forms being his chief source of inspiration. He paid Mackmurdo the compliment of using one of his wallpapers in this house. Horta designed other important buildings in Brussels: the Hotel van Etvelde in 1898, the Hotel Solvay and the Maison du Peuple in 1895–1900. The latter is remarkable for its façade of iron and glass.

Another Belgian, Henri van de Velde (1863–1957), was not lacking in courage himself in rejecting nineteenth-century cultural pastiche. Starting as a painter he soon displayed an interest in furniture, house decoration, tapestry, silver and jewelry. Throughout his work he strictly followed the tenet that the nature of the material must determine the form and the decoration of whatever subject was involved.

It was from France, pioneer of so many world-affecting art forms, that there came some of the most sophisticated and eccentric manifestations of Art Nouveau. The name of the Movement was finally settled in the French tongue and many of its foremost artists and architects took up the new style. They, of all artists, caught Walter Crane's definition of Art Nouveau as a 'disease' in its most virulent form. Paris

BELOW *Satinwood cabinet with inset painted panels, designed by E. W. Godwin, about 1877. In this piece, Godwin mixes Japonisme with romantic medievalism.*

became one of the centres for this newest of crazes and either excelled in it or descended to producing artifacts at their most impractical and bizarre.

The Paris Exhibition of 1900 marked the height of the capital's power and influence; from this moment it reigned supreme in the *Modern Style*, outdoing nearly all others in the way it had always done.

But not even the French could deny their debt to England and Morris. Not that Paris had the monopoly of French talent: Nancy was also an important centre, producing, among others, such designers as Majorelle, the Daum Brothers and Emile Gallé. It was the latter, who, as early as 1872, visited England and drank from the inspirational fountain of the Arts and Crafts Movement. Equipped with this, his native sensitivity, and expertise inherited from a father who owned a pottery workshop, he set about perfecting a technique of glass making which was to influence strongly the course of Art Nouveau. In this, the design was covered with wax and the remaining areas eaten with acid, which achieved a double surface, both matt and shiny. This glass, with its myriad variations of colour and shading, resulting from cutting, was the very apotheosis of mystery. Greens and yellows, rose and brown, violet and orange: all the variations of smoke from thick to thin, transfigured and illuminated his vases, glasses and jugs.

Louis Majorelle followed Gallé, working in the tradition of French furniture design and enriching it with his particular contribution of convoluted and twisted Art Nouveau shapes often carried out in gilt and bronze. He made wood and metal suit his whims but he was always the master, never the servant, of his materials.

One of the most famous and most easily recognizable products of Art Nouveau are the Metro entrances in Paris which date from 1900. These were designed by Hector Guimard, one of the most interesting of French architects and designers. He was influenced by Horta but gave his work a special flavour inspired, as was Horta, by plant forms. His first principal architectural venture was the Castel Béranger built in Paris between 1894 and 1898. The building boasts a staircase as bold as Horta's but it is in the iron gateway that Guimard's genius is shown to full advantage.

In 1895, Samuel Bing, a collector of Japanese art, opened a shop in Paris which he called *La Maison de l'Art Nouveau*. Henri van de Velde is credited with coining the phrase in 1894 but it was Bing's new shop, to which so many artists flocked, that gave the Movement its official title.

It is in the realm of jewelry that Art Nouveau holds unquestioned excellence, and it is French designers such as Vever, Fouquet and above all, René Lalique, who produced the best work. Gold, obsidian, pearls, opals, enamel, diamonds, rubies, *plique à jour* and even carved glass were grist to his exotic mill. Myriads of necklaces, brooches, hair ornaments, pendants, combs and pins spun from his fertile brain. He was taken up by Bernhardt, lionized by society

Honesty, a plant with purple flowers and transparent, fragile seed pods, was much beloved by Art Nouveau designers. The pale greeny pods spiral up the side of a silver and gold vase produced at the Loezt factory.

and given awards. He used every plant form; every insect and every strange creature from snake to bat; he rendered women's faces, breasts and hair. He gave solid and glittering form to such soft natural forms as the convolvulus, honesty, sycamore seeds and thistledown.

It is strange that from Scotland, geographically and in many ways culturally, remote from Europe, that there should emerge one of the most interesting and important exponents of the Movement. Largely ignored by England he was nevertheless hailed on the Continent as one of the most important exponents of the New Style. This man was Charles Rennie Mackintosh, architect, furniture designer, painter, jeweller, *et al.*

Living in Glasgow he founded a famous group: 'The Four', consisting of himself, his wife Margaret, Margaret Macdonald and her sister Frances. This group was acknowledged by the Vienna *Sezessionstil* and exhibited there in 1897. The group also held an important exhibition at Turin in 1901. Rejecting the florid, over-rich curvilinear motifs common to most of Art Nouveau, Mackintosh and his associates went in for sound structure, simplicity, long straight lines, organized space and such cool colours as white, mauve, green and grey, often emphasized by black.

Apart from many private houses, Mackintosh designed three buildings which are now most closely connected with his name. All in Glasgow, these are the School of Art, the Willow Tea Rooms and Miss Cranston's Tea Room. Of these, only the Art School, with its magnificent 17-ft high library, remains in its entirety.

His Willow Tea Rooms was a masterpiece of design, with its white wooden doors panelled in multi-coloured glass and metal. For these rooms he designed everything: chairs, tables, carpets, light fittings as well as the murals. Today only the remarkable pair of doors remains.

Mackintosh was particularly appreciated in Vienna where he exhibited interiors at the eighth Sezessionist Exhibition. Austria and Germany had been slow starters in the new Style. But the magazine *Jugend* gave Art Nouveau one of its other names: *Jugendstil*. Van de Velde lectured on the new art form at Krefeld in 1895, exhibited his own work at Dresden in 1897 and, when he moved to Berlin in 1899, he became an acknowledged leader of the Sezessionists.

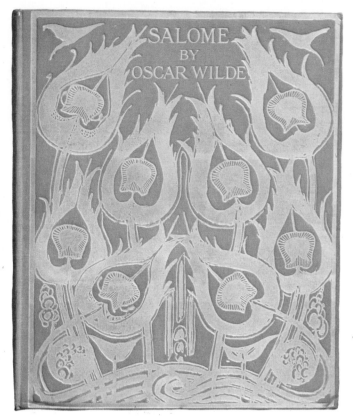

In Germany, Hermann Obrist was an artist who practised and propagated Art Nouveau. He designed a revolutionary wall hanging and went on to ceramics and sculpture, creating abstract whirls and spirals out of stone and clay. Influenced by Tiffany and Gallé, the Germans also turned their attention to glass, and Johann Lötz most nearly resembled these two masters.

Most people have heard of Tiffany – his lamps, those stained-glass mushrooms, have become almost an Art Nouveau cliché. Son of a successful New York jeweller who had a branch of his shop in Regent Street, in London, in 1868, the young Tiffany often visited it and it was during this time that he was influenced by Ruskin and Morris.

Back in New York he decorated many houses for the new American rich but it was not until the late 1890s that he began to work with glass in a way which was to make him famous. In 1880 he patented *Favrile* glass, an iridescent technique made by exposing hot glass to a series of metallic fumes and oxides. Soon it was extremely popular and imitations were produced but never with Tiffany's unique flair and craftsmanship. He produced a vast amount of delicate, exotic and imaginative vases, glasses and lamps. In 1892 he exhibited a stained-glass window in Europe which guaranteed his influence and fame on the

Continent and it was inevitable that the perceptive Samuel Bing should include Tiffany as one of his biggest exhibitors in his new shop. Despite many followers in America, Tiffany remained the only really original Art Nouveau artist in the decorative field that America produced. It was left to the architect Louis Sullivan to give American architecture a particularly Art Nouveau look. In the manner of Mackintosh he used light, simple assemblages of lines and curves. He worked with exposed cast iron and his decorative motifs were drawn from Celtic and Byzantine sources.

147

The Care of Antiques

While describing the best environment for antiques and best methods for cleaning them, the following should not be taken as a do-it-yourself guide. Precious things in need of repair or restoration should be entrusted to an expert.

Having invested love and money into the possession of antiques, it is important that these investments have long-term value. Enjoyment and care are compatible. Given an understanding of the natural causes of deterioration of antiques, care becomes a simple matter of common sense. Preventive conservation is the term used for this course of action. Restoration is expensive, sometimes impossible, and, far too frequently, avoidable. This chapter will discuss various common causes of deterioration, steps for their prevention and some information about cure. Cause and effect are stressed because this is the source and sign of the problem of deterioration. Restoration and its highly skilled methods are involved topics upon which expert advice or attention should be sought. Some knowledge, however, of what can be done is essential for the potential buyer or owner faced with something needing repair.

THE CAUSES OF DETERIORATION

The factors which influence deterioration are simple to understand and control. These factors will be discussed first and then their application to different materials handled under separate headings.

Relative humidity and temperature Relative humidity is probably the most important single factor to control in preventive conservation. It sets the limits for most deterioration processes. Unfortunately, it is a difficult term to explain. In formula form:

Relative humidity (or RH) =
$$\frac{\text{absolute humidity}}{\text{saturation humidity}} \times 100$$

In simple terms this is the relationship of the amount of moisture actually in the air to the maximum amount of moisture possible in the air at a given temperature. In practical terms it is a measurement of the amount of moisture available. It is related to temperature: raising and lowering the temperature decreases and increases respectively the available moisture. A high RH value means a high moisture content while a low RH means little available moisture is present in the air. Most materials try to come to equilibrium with the environment, absorbing or releasing moisture. Problems occur when they have to adjust too quickly or when the moisture content becomes too high or too low.

There are two ways of controlling relative humidity. The amount of moisture present in the air can be altered, keeping the temperature constant, by using humidifiers or dehumidifiers set for specific RH levels. The alternative is to alter the temperature gradually – increased warmth decreases the RH and decreased heat increases the RH. Relative humidity can be measured using a hygrometer where absolute values are desired.

Light Bright light and ultra-violet rays lead to fading and other degradation. Daylight and most fluorescent light is harmful. Light levels are normally given in 'lux' which is a measure of light intensity for a given area. Absolute values are difficult to judge without a lux-meter. Materials subject to fading require low levels of light (50 lux). As permanence increases so can the allowable amounts of light. Common sense must be the guide.

Heat The relationship of heat to relative humidity and moisture content has been discussed. Heat in itself can cause problems. Some materials can soften and distort. Blistering can occur. Stresses can be set up and distortion can result.

Atmospheric pollution Dust and dirt are all too common a cause of deterioration. In addition to spoiling the appearance of fine things, they are a source of abrasion and encourage harmful chemical reactions. Airborne sulphides prevalent in urban atmospheres lead to tarnishing and acid formation.

Inherent instability Under the term inherent instability are included such problems as salts, stresses, and acidity. These can usually be controlled by environmental factors. They may also be made worse by faulty restoration or handling.

Insects and mould growth Organic materials such as textiles, leather, paper and wood are susceptible to biological attack. Environmental factors are contributory, but contamination is the immediate source.

Physical damage Any antique subject to use and handling is prone to disaster. Some wear and tear is inevitable and should be viewed as part of historical ageing. Carelessness, however, is inexcusable. Antiques lose strength with age and fragility should be taken into account before handling, not after. Restoration is no panacea.

Restoration Restoration must be included under deterioration because of the conservation ethics involved. All restoration must be viewed as a temporary measure. Potential problems resulting from restoration and repair must be minimized or eliminated. Where possible, restoration should be reversible, without harming the original fabric. Added substances should be compatible in every way. Stresses and instability must not be induced. Finally, the degree of restoration must be decided – that is, should the aim be to restore the object's original appearance or should allowances for age be made.

METALS

Silver Silver corrosion or 'tarnish' is usually in the form of silver sulphide and is mainly caused by a polluted atmosphere containing hydrogen sulphide. The point must be made that decaying organic matter, vulcanized rubber (beware of rubber bands), certain paints and textiles, and eggs can be a source and cause damage. Silver that has been debased with copper and silver plate may well show evidence of copper corrosion.

There are many proprietary silver cleaners available and these fall into the categories of abrasives and chemical cleaners or a combination of the two. Strongly abrasive metal polishes should be avoided or used with care, as silver is a soft metal and vigorous or frequent cleaning will wear away detail. They are indeed useful for attacking especially resistant areas of tarnish, but should be used locally and with a soft cotton swab. Most good polishes made specifically for silver cleaning are safe enough if used according to the instructions. Commercially available tarnish solvents, i.e., the type in which the silver is cleaned by dipping, should be approached with some caution. After frequent use, these solvents contain a fair amount of silver in solution which tends to plate on to the surface of the metal being cleaned. This gives it a slightly frosted appearance, which must then be removed by polishing. Also, these dipping cleaners remove all silver sulphide, so that detail and engraved lines lose the contrast they would have had if left tarnished. A further precaution must be made when cleaning silver objects such as jewelry with pearls or coral, or knives with mother-of-pearl handles, as these solvent cleaners contain an acid which can cause serious damage. On the positive side, however, solvent cleaners can be used to reduce the amount of abrasion needed for stubborn tarnish and can often be the only method for cleaning *inside* objects, in inaccessible places, and for silver chains. Copper corrosion on silver can usually be removed with standard silver cleaning procedures. Extensive or resistant corrosion can be removed with either concentrated ammonia or 30% formic acid solution applied locally on cotton swabs.

After cleaning and degreasing, silver may be lacquered with a nitro-cellulose lacquer free of sulphides. Where silver is not being lacquered, and this applies to silver intended for use and subjected to handling, it is advisable to keep tarnish to a minimum. Some polishes have tarnish prohibitors. Silver should be stored sensibly and not in contact with such sources of sulphides as mentioned above and protected from atmospheric pollution as much as possible. Cloth bags and impregnated papers designed for silver storage are available. Beware of plastic bags for storage. Although these are excellent barriers against the atmosphere, there is the danger that some types may deteriorate in time releasing sulphides and adhering to the surface of the silver.

Gold The beauty of gold from the conservator's point of view is, alas, practical, not aesthetic, for it does not corrode. It does, however, get dirty, but responds beautifully to gentle cleaning with mild soap and water. Where copper is present in a gold-copper alloy, it is possible to get a slight tarnishing, but this is easily removed by cleaning with a mild polish. Copper corrosion can be found on antiquities or on gilt brass and this is best removed with concentrated ammonia or 30% formic acid applied locally with a cotton swab.

Lead, Pewter and Tin The important thing to remember about lead, tin and pewter, an alloy of the first two, is that these are amphoteric metals, that is, they are attacked by both acids and alkali. This fact must be borne in mind in cleaning and stabilizing techniques and also in subsequent usage. This is the reason why antique pewter can be a source of lead poisoning when used with acidic food-stuffs such as vinegar. Electrolytic and chemical reduction are available for treating heavily corroded specimens in the laboratory and are best carried out by trained people under these conditions. Antique pewterware is usually tarnished a mellow grey colour. There is no need to remove this layer as the appearance can be improved with a soft wax polish. Should a more metallic surface or highlights be desired, a mild metal polish is effective. These metals are usually given a protective coat of wax.

The storage of lead and pewter must be considered. Because these metals can be readily attacked by organic acid vapours, cupboards and shelves of oak, fir and some other woods should be avoided. The same holds true for cardboard boxes.

Copper and Brass Copper and brass can be dealt with separately from bronzes and other metals found in antiquities. Obviously there are copper and brass antiquities and the same problems apply, but this section deals rather with non-archaeological material. It should be pointed out that bronze disease is not a condition confined only to antiquities or bronze: any copper containing metal subjected to chloride contamination and high humidity is at risk.

For the most part, brass and copper cleaning is simply a matter of removing a darkened layer of oxide tarnish. Commercially prepared chemical solvents, abrasives and combination preparations are available. Cleaning can be very difficult, but hard work is often the best answer. Short cuts can be disastrous. Wire brushes, coarse wire wool, and glass paper can produce scratching. Chemical cleaners can cause copper plating on the surface of brass. Brass and copper are often lacquered, and this can become darkened or scratched. A sensible first step in cleaning would be to examine the surface for a lacquer, as its removal will greatly facilitate cleaning. Acetone is a good general solvent for lacquers, but, in some cases, only the rather drastic application of paint stripper will do the trick. Where these metals have been painted or coated with heavy sooty grimes, a paint stripper may again be necessary as a first step. Soaking in an ammonia solution or its local application is another short cut where the tarnish is especially resistant or where other copper corrosion products are present. It can, however, overclean, and any residue of ammonia can lead to a bluish bloom in recesses which can be difficult to remove. A mixture of salt and lemon juice is said to be a good cleaner, but common sense would identify it as abrasive and a deliberate exposure to a source of chlorides.

Brass and copper are relatively easy to care for. Avoid prolonged contact with vinegar and waxy materials which can lead to the formation of verdigris. Lacquering is often done to eliminate repeated cleaning.

JEWELRY

Jewelry Although this chapter has been set out to deal with materials rather than artifacts, it might be of value to discuss jewelry as a subject because of the wide range of materials which commonly come together under this heading, and the problems to be faced in any treatment, care and usage. The cleaning and care of gold and silver have been covered. Acceptable treatments as described for the metals involved in jewelry settings may be followed, so long as such treatments are totally compatible with stones, adhesives or other materials involved. This is very important and will be covered in some detail.

Where adhesives have been used, solvent cleaning (even with water) can be risky and may be avoided by using a dry soft brush for cleaning. The uncontrolled use of solvent could also damage hair as in mourning brooches, photographs or miniatures. Where a stone has been set using metal claws or other mechanical settings, the article can be cleaned with a mild detergent and warm water using a soft brush. It is then rinsed well and polished with a soft cloth – care being taken not to catch and damage prongs. Some grime may require a stronger solvent like methylated spirits applied in the same way. The commercially prepared jewelry cleaners which are available may be useful, but attention should be paid to the instructions. Avoid the temptation to scrape away resistant deposits with a pin as scratches can result. The tightening of stones and any reshaping of metal is best left to jewellers.

Organic materials used in jewelry must be considered. Generally they are affected by heat, water and abrasion. Mother-of-pearl, pearls, coral and shell cannot be cleaned in any acidic solvent. Tortoise-shell and horn cannot be subjected to excess water. Ivory and bone are damaged by heat and water. Amber can be dissolved by spirit solvents. All these materials are best cleaned by surface cleaning with cotton wool dampened in a dilute non-ionic detergent. A mildly abrasive cream polish may be needed in some cases. A finish with microcrystalline wax will not only offer some protection, but will improve the surface and appearance.

Most gemstones are non-reactive and present little problem on cleaning. Turquoise and opals are porous and can change colour through careless handling. They are affected by heat, detergents and oils. Also opals tend to be soft and easily scratched. Some stones such as emeralds and topaz can be accidently broken if struck along a cleavage line. A competent jeweller can give advice about the care of stones.

GLASS

During burial, glasses, enamels, and pottery glazes may undergo a leaching out of some of their ingredients from the surface yielding a peeling film or iridescent surface. In the case of glass of antiquity, this may be considered aesthetically pleasing and its preservation desired. A light coat of 5% alcoholic solution of soluble nylon is usually sufficient to consolidate this surface without spoiling its colour and beauty. With glazes and enamels this same iridescence may be masking design underneath and it can be removed by careful polishing, or reduced with a lacquer or suitable resin. 'Weeping

glass' is another fault found in some antique glass and is caused by an inherent shortage of lime used in its manufacture. This prevents a leaching out of alkalis during periods of high humidity with the resultant formation of beads of alkali solution and incrustation on the surface. The only cure is one of preventive conservation – the objects must be kept in an environment of low humidity (below 40% RH).

'Glass fatigue' is a term which may, or may not, have substance. By this is meant that as glass ages, strength and resilience is lost. Composition of the glass and its subsequent history are contributing factors. The point to be made is that glass is unpredictable and a certain element of risk is present when any restoration is attempted. Glasses react badly to sudden changes in temperature and crack, craze or break. For this reason, care should be taken when washing glass, using hot liquids, or friction.

Glass may be polished with a gentle metal polish and a soft cloth to remove light surface films. Scratches can likewise be removed though more buffing may be needed. This might best be left to the experienced restorer. Chipped edges can be ground down but the risk of breakage is sufficient to warrant leaving this task to experts. A ground and re-polished rim can usually be detected by the fact that the original somewhat swollen lip is lost on grinding down.

Washing in a solution of ammonia in warm water followed by polishing with a soft cloth can be very effective. Methylated spirit on a soft cloth can also be used. Care should be taken when cleaning mirrors and picture glasses not to wet frames or allow the cleaning solution to get to the underside of the glass. Some residues, especially those found inside containers, may prove difficult to shift. Lime deposits in water vessels may be dissolved by a prolonged soaking in distilled water. Dilute hydrochloric acid may have to be used. Hydrogen peroxide may shift organic stains.

Repairs of glass range from the difficult to the impossible. Unless an adhesive is used which is completely colourless and has a refractive index close to that of glass, the join will be obvious. A further complication is the fact that glass is non-porous and the adhesive has nothing on which to key. New adhesives are constantly being put forth for glass restoration, and a simple and ideal adhesive will no doubt be found. In the meantime, a nitro-cellulose-based adhesive would be advisable as it is easy to use, is easily reversed, and will hold the object together. Glass restorers make use of certain epoxy resins specially formulated for glass repair and for making up missing areas, but here again experience is necessary. Chipped and damaged enamels can also be repaired with epoxy and acrylic resins.

CERAMICS

Deterioration and damage to pottery can take many forms. Some knowledge of each and its cure should give an insight into the care of pottery.

Pots which have been buried for a long period of time, or more modern pots, by certain usage, may be saturated with salts. On exposure to high humidity, these salts go into solution and migrate toward the surface. Crystallization occurs with a drop in humidity and the result is a physical breaking apart of the surface as these crystals grow. Glazes and painted decoration can be permanently destroyed. The usual treatment is prolonged washing in constantly changing tap or distilled water until tests show the pot to be free of salts. In some cases consolidation may be needed.

Buried pottery may also have a surface contaminated by concretions of lime, gypsum, or siliceous materials which may be unsightly or obscure the decoration. These deposits can be removed by mechanical means such as with a scalpel or vibrotool or with acids. Acid treatment on pottery should not be lightly undertaken as the pottery itself is liable to destruction. Also soluble salts are formed and these must be removed. Advice should be sought before embarking on this kind of treatment.

Glazes are a form of glass and behave in much the same way. A cracked glaze or crazing may be formed on manufacture where the pot and the glaze have a different coefficient of contraction. Crazing can be caused by improper use. Sudden temperature change, as occurs when warming plates or putting them in hot water can be a cause. Heat methods of re-glazing in ceramic restoration can also create these glaze cracks. Once a glaze is crazed, dirt and stains can get through and be difficult to remove.

The body of the ceramic itself can be extremely fragile and is subject to breakage, chipping, and cracks. This may be due to poor handling, too rapid expansion or contraction, or pressure as in stacking or burial. Once cracked or broken, pottery becomes increasingly fragile. Edges chip and become stained and dirty. Cracks allow stains to creep under the glaze. Bits of glaze become lost. Even with the utmost care, pieces can be lost. It would be advisable to wrap carefully all pieces to avoid further damage and put them safely away until restoration can be carried out. Even tiny pieces should be saved.

Methods of ceramic restoration are too involved to be discussed here in sufficient detail. However, some information about the subject would be useful. Cleaning the pieces and cracks is the first consideration and this may entail removing old repairs. The choice of solvent is dictated by the kind of material being removed. Thorough cleaning is essential as edges darkened with stains or dirt, or coated with adhesive, make for bad and visible joins. Soaking in a bleaching solution of hydrogen peroxide and ammonia is best for stain removal, as such a solution leaves no residue to form future problems, as can be the case with commercial bleaches based on chlorine.

The choice of adhesive is the next consideration. It is usually advisable to use an adhesive which is reversible in an organic solvent. Animal glue and natural resins have been used in the past but become dark, brittle and nearly insoluble on ageing. Impact adhesives tend to be too thick or difficult to use. A nitro-cellulose adhesive is suitable for most purposes, as it has excellent ageing properties and is easy to use and remove. Professional ceramic restorers may prefer a stronger adhesive such as an epoxy resin, but remember that such adhesives are difficult to remove when set and poor sticking may be difficult to correct.

Riveting pieces together has been popular in the past as a strong method of repair, but in recent years better adhesives have tended to replace it in restoration. Unsightly rivets lying across a join draw the eye to the imperfection. They can be removed and the join restuck using a modern adhesive, but the restorer is faced with not only perfecting a join but also a series of holes to fill and match in.

Missing parts of pottery can be made up using a number of methods and materials. Plaster of Paris is very common but is not overly strong. Epoxy resins with fillers are stronger. These require casting or supporting prior to hardening. Instruction is essential. Attention should be paid to getting a surface of the correct texture and level as the body of the pot. Made-up areas can be coloured to tone in with the rest of the pot or coloured to match exactly the part which they replace. The finish can be matched with lacquers, waxes and glazes. Perhaps the best match for ceramic glazes can be obtained using a heat-cured glaze which is sprayed on to avoid build-up and brush strokes. Mends and replaced parts can be virtually indistinguishable. It is bad practice to carry restoration over the original and legitimate surface. This is often done in an attempt to disguise restoration but, on ageing, may make the repair appear larger and more obvious than in fact it is. Marvellous restoration of ceramics is possible but is involved and difficult and is best done by trusted restorers.

Most restoration can be easily detected on close examination. In a good light look for differences in the surface texture and plane. Discrepancies in colour indicate an inexact colour match or colour change on ageing. The colour on restored parts may be near the surface while the original surface may have a clear glaze of some depth. Restored areas often have a different feel. Most restoration shows up clearly when viewed under ultra-violet light.

A few final points about restoration of ceramics should be made. Any restoration will age at a different rate from the original. Ageing can be accelerated by such factors as light, heat and moisture. The use to which a ceramic is to be put should be taken into account when the type and extent of restoration is being considered. Museum restoration techniques may not stand up to daily domestic requirements but would be adequate for ornamental use.

TEXTILES

It might be argued that of all the materials being discussed here, textiles are the most vulnerable yet severely treated. If properly cared for, they can be kept in excellent condition and last for centuries. Under adverse conditions, the deterioration can be alarmingly rapid.

Insect attack is probably the most rapid form of damage, and moth the most obvious culprit. Although flying adults, eggs and pupae are found on affected textiles, the damage is done by the larvae. They attack wool, but will eat through other types of fibre to get at it. Carpet beetles and fur beetles are also problems. Even woodworm and silver-fish will eat through textiles on their way to or from a food source.

Most insect attack occurs during storage, when the larvae can develop and feed undisturbed in dark and still conditions. Some insects pupate in textiles, secreting a corrosive substance about the pupal case. Carpets covered by furniture and deep folds in drapery produce a similar environment. Food stains can provide an added enticement. Frequent inspection, cleanliness, and airing are essential.

Once the damage has been done, there is no cure other than tedious repair. Preventive measures are the answer. An insecticide must be included with textiles in storage. Naphthalene (moth balls) has been successfully used for years. Para-dichlorobenzene crystals may be preferred as the odour is not so lingering. Both are effective. The advisability of contact between textiles and these crystals has been questioned as bleaching may occur. A sensible precaution would be to place the insecticide inside a cloth or polythene bag with breathing holes to allow the vapour and not the crystals to reach the textile.

Air-borne dust and dirt can cause damage as well as being unsightly. Grit gets into the fibres and acts as an abrasive to wear down strength. Flexibility is reduced. Dust particles are hydroscopic – they attract moisture, which can hasten biological and chemical deterioration. Much of this can be removed with light vacuuming. For delicate textiles it may be necessary to protect fibres with a piece of net to prevent the suction from lifting loose threads.

Too high a humidity can also cause problems and encourage mould growth. On the other hand, too low a humidity level leads to textiles drying out and fibres becoming embrittled. An ideal RH level for textiles lies in the region of 50 to 60%.

Most early dyes used in textiles are subject to fading. Naturally, some dyes are less stable than others. Often two or more were used to produce a final colour and one of these may fade more quickly. Such is often the case with greens, where yellow and blue dyes were used and the yellow has disappeared. The major cause of fading is light, and evidence seems to show that intensity and ultra-violet rays are the offensive elements. In museums attempts are made to eliminate all ultra-violet light rays by excluding daylight and then by using artificial light sources proven free of ultra-violet. Light levels for textiles are kept to below 50 lux. In the home, this would be more difficult, but it should be possible to keep prized textiles out of direct sunlight and as protected from bright light as possible. Except for special low U.V. tubes, fluorescent light is dangerous.

Physical damage through wear and tear should be kept to the minimum by avoiding excess wear and protecting vulnerable areas. Wall-mounted textiles are best hung using velcro-strip, as the weight is evenly distributed across the entire top of the textile rather than isolated points. Strain and distortion are reduced accordingly.

Atmospheric pollution, especially sulphides, leads to problems of a more chemical nature. Fabrics can increase in acidity and degradation accelerated. Metallic threads become tarnished. Some dyes, mainly with browns and black, are acidic in themselves and fibres dyed with them deteriorate rapidly. These problems are difficult to deal with and advice should be sought.

Cleaning can be straightforward. However, there are sufficient exceptions to warrant extreme caution. Not all dyes are fast for a start. Once colours have run, it can be extremely difficult to put things right. Some fabrics are too weak for standard cleaning procedures. Attempts at removing stains can remove colours and fabric in the bargain. In short, cleaning can be a risk unless done by experienced people. Always have a test done on each colour to establish the best method before any cleaning is carried out.

Textile restorers prefer to clean as gently as possible. Soaking in cold distilled water is used where possible. Where detergent is needed, a 0·5 to 1% solution of a non-ionic detergent is used with careful rinsing, again in distilled water, at the end of treatment. Delicate fabrics may require supporting during washing. While damp, fibres are more flexible and can be aligned. In cases where textiles are incompatible with water, other methods can be used. Tri- and dichloroethylene are used, or 'dry cleaning' with a powder such as a mixture of powdered magnesia and potato flour.

Extremely fragile textiles may require supporting. Crepeline, tertal, or fine terylene net are commonly used. The supporting fabric is attached by stitches or the net may be impregnated with a thermo-plastic re-versible synthetic resin adhesive and attached by ironing. Again this is really specialized work.

A final point about textile care should be made. Textiles should be stored in such a way that creases are kept to a minimum. This is especially true with silks. Fibres are encouraged to break where sharp folds are permitted. Acid-free tissue paper can be used to round out folds. Large flat textiles are best rolled. Avoid prolonged contact with acid-containing substances such as cardboard. Finally, watch out for insects and mould.

LEATHER

Leather plays an important part in antiques. It can be found in book-bindings, costume, furniture and small artifacts. Its appearance can be improved and its life prolonged by care and preventive conservation measures. The protein fibres of leather provide a source of nutrition for insects which burrow through causing incredible damage both to the appearance and the strength of the object. With books, the paper may be the main attraction and the leather binding just the dessert – the same may be true of furniture. With small objects the pests can be exterminated by sealing the infested object in a polythene bag containing para-dichlorobenzene crystals at room temperature for at least two weeks. With larger objects professional attention is advised.

Mould growth can occur when leather is subjected to high humidity. The best solution is simply to increase ventilation and reduce the humidity level to a safe value (RH 50–60%). When dry, remove the mould by gentle brushing. Resist the temptation to dry leather too rapidly with excess heat: it can shrink and become brittle.

Contact with water may damage leather by removing certain protective elements. Semi-tanned leathers can undergo incredible shrinking on drying following contact with water.

The other extreme can be equally dangerous. Leather subjected to very dry atmospheres or heat lose moisture content to the extent that they lose flexibility and crack and break. For this reason, leather-bound books should not be placed over radiators and the like.

Though perhaps not as light-sensitive as textiles, leather (especially if dyed), is subject to fading and degradation accelerated by light. Again ultra-violet light and high intensity are to blame. Safe levels by museum standards are around 150 lux though may be lower for some dyes. Sensible avoidance is the best course of action.

Leather covered furniture suffers from wear and tear – table and desk tops more from abuse. Rings left from glasses, cigarette burns and deep scrapes are all too common and all too easy to avoid. A good wax may help. Microcrystalline-wax-based preparations are available and in addition to being strong are somewhat waterproof.

Wax will help to improve the appearance of any leather and give some protection. The British Museum has developed a leather dressing containing lanoline, beeswax, cedarwood oil and a solvent of hexane or trichloroethane. There is a similar preparation which is commercially available. This can be rubbed into the leather to increase pliability and replaces natural oils lost on ageing. The instructions should be carefully followed as too liberal an application can produce a sticky surface.

PAPER

Any treatment of paper is only for the trained and experienced specialist. It is too complex a substance for simple remedies. Preventive conservation will be invaluable.

One of the most common blemishes found on prints and drawings is 'foxing' (discoloration). This is almost certainly caused by mould growth. It is quite frequently found where prints have been framed and a micro-environment, free of ventilation, exists between the glass and the paper. Situations of high humidity obviously encourage the disorder, but it is possible to have the existence of a greater RH in this tiny space than that of the room at large. Mounts increase the width of this space between the glass and paper and reduce the problem. High humidity should be avoided. Moving framed prints from a cool outside wall may also help. Paper restorers can bleach out foxing by using vapours.

Silver-fish are the major insect problems. They are mainly attracted to starch and sizes used in paper. Woodworm and other wood-boring beasts are after the cellulose. Books are a source of food in themselves, while with prints and drawings it is usually the back-board and frame they are after. Paradichlorobenzene may be used as a fumigant as described for leather.

Prints and, most notably, watercolours can be quickly faded by light. In addition, light can accelerate paper deterioration. The acceptable ceiling in museums is 50 lux light intensity with the exclusion of all ultra-violet rays. In the home, avoid direct sunlight and indeed, reduce daylight as much as possible. Fluorescent light should be free of ultra-violet.

Excess heat and low relative humidity can cause paper to dry out and become embrittled. Chemical factors of ageing are accelerated, and the paper turns yellow.

When having prints and drawings framed, it is advisable to insist on the use of conservation board for mounts and as an isolating layer between the print and the back-board. Conservation board is acid free and avoids the problem of acidic contamination which is possible where ordinary cardboard, wood or hardboard are in contact with paper.

WOOD

Of the organic materials discussed here, wood is the most common in the home. Long prized for its strength, beauty and flexibility, it has been a major element in furniture manufacture, ornament and house construction. Given reasonable care, its life and beauty can be ageless. Conversely, its destruction can be alarmingly quick.

Wood is seasoned to be in equilibrium with a given environment. The moisture content of the material is self-adjusting to that of the atmosphere surrounding it. Moisture is absorbed and released as required. Too sudden or extreme a demand results in stress, often with severe damage. An ideal situation would be a constant RH in the zone of 50–60% at a temperature of 20°C (68°F). Central heating tends to produce a warm but dry atmosphere. Rapid temperature changes and thus, the rise and fall in RH, cause too rapid an adjustment of the part of wood. This can happen with sporadic heating or opening windows or doors to cool rooms. Locally applied factors should also be noted such as wetting wood or extremely drying situations such as near radiators or fires. These moisture-related forms of damage can be manifested in different ways.

Shrinkage is a result of loss of volume as moisture is removed. Some shrinkage is acceptable as part of the normal equilibrium process and is naturally reversible when moisture increases. A critical point is reached, however, where so much moisture is removed that the walls of cells making up the wood structure collapse. Strength is decreased. As still more moisture is lost, splitting occurs. When moisture becomes available again, it is absorbed with an increase in volume on the part of the wood and cracks may move together. However, the damage done to the cell walls is irreversible, and the overall volume remains decreased. Structural strength is likewise reduced. Further exposure to drying conditions continues the process with perhaps even greater ease. Eventually, noticeable cracks and splints appear reaching such proportions that they must remain as permanent voids. Not only is strength and beauty hampered but distortion through warping and breakage can occur. Joins can break and veneers lift.

Where cracks are indeed small they may be closed on correcting the RH of the environment. Adhesives may be successful at permanently holding cracks and splits together, but the risk is run of forcing the strain to seek a new outlet and splits may occur elsewhere. Bad shrinkage cracks are normally filled. A sliver of a similar wood with grain running in the same direction can be shaped and fitted into the split with an adhesive. This replaces the lost volume of wood, should behave in a similar manner to that wood and can skilfully be toned in to match. Other fillers can be used. A mixture of sawdust and glue is common, as are commercially prepared wood fillers. A word of warning should be given. Where any material is inserted into a split, it should expand and contract in the same way as the wood being replaced and should not be of a harder substance. A hard inflexible filler could act like a wedge and increase the problem.

Swelling is the opposite problem and is caused by too much moisture in the wood. Pressure is exerted on joins, drawers and doors stick, and inlay disrupted. Drying out may produce other stresses. Excessive movement in wood in either direction is bad. Swollen wood should be dried slowly to an acceptable level. Mould can also occur with high humidity.

The third moisture-related damage is warping. Wood is not a perfectly homogeneous substance. It is made up of cells of different structures, functions and lying in different directions. Each type responds differently to moisture. Uncontrolled levels of RH lead to twisting and warping. Wax or polish is often applied to only one side of a piece of wood thereby sealing that surface. Its opposite surface is then more available to influence by moisture, and can shrink or swell more than the protected side. Curling is the result. With furniture it is common to have different RH levels on each surface of the wood, i.e. a box or chest of drawers with one moisture level inside and another outside. A constant and controlled RH level (50–60%) is the best method of prevention. Where wood is warped it can be straightened by steam processes or temporary exposure to high humidity and then using the moisture-induced flexibility to reshape the wood. It is held in this position and brought slowly back to an acceptable moisture content. Support may be needed to prevent the warp recurring. As finishes are endangered and new stresses applied, it is best to avoid treatment.

The second major cause of wood deterioration is insect attack. The common furniture beetle, *Anobium punctatum*, is the species most often encountered. The larvae of this beetle (woodworm) will attack almost any type of wood. The adult beetle is free-flying but rarely noticed. Most damage is done beneath the surface in the form of a network of channels eaten away by the larvae. Flight holes are made in the surface by the adult on emergence from the wood. Holes indicate that the wood has been attacked at some time past or present. Fresh powdery bore dust falling from the holes implies infestation is active. Powder post beetle is similar but less common. Unfortunately the ideal environmental conditions for wood are also ideal for insects.

Control can be by several methods. Fumigation on a large scale must be done commercially. Small objects can be fumigated by keeping the object in a sealed container with paradichlorobenzene crystals for several weeks. Commercially prepared woodworm killing fluids can be used, and these not only kill living woodworm but offer protection for years. Before any treatment, it is essential to make sure that no harm will be done to the finish. Instructions should give a clue, but first test in a small and inconspicuous area, for these fluids can cause some darkening and staining. Take care to prevent the fluid from touching textiles or upholstery. In such cases, professional fumigation may be the only solution. All the wooden surfaces of the infected article should be treated. The insecticide is brushed on, making sure that all cracks and crevices are reached. The bottom under-surfaces of legs etc., should not be overlooked. Inject fluid into holes to ensure deep penetration. After treatment the holes can be filled with pigmented wax. This improves the appearance, and makes new holes immediately obvious.

Since light can fade wood or change the colours and attractive contrasts can be lost, bright sunlight should be avoided.

Repairs to wooden objects can be simple. Joins break down due to wood movement, natural embrittlement of glue, insect or mould attack of glue or physical strain. Before resticking, all old glue must be removed to ensure a good join. Animal glue will come down in warm water, care being taken not to wet the finish if refinishing is not desired. Other solvents may be required for different adhesives. Usually, it is best to use the same adhesive as has been used throughout the piece so that all joins will behave in a similar manner and to simplify future restoration. Apply adhesives to both surfaces to ensure a complete bond before sticking the pieces together. Clamps are often needed to ensure a tight fit. Excess glue is best removed before drying to give a cleaner appearance.

With breaks, and by this is meant not-intentional joins, the choice of adhesives is wider. A good-working adhesive giving strength and more permanence may be selected. Sticking is much the same as with joins. Sometimes dowelling or new wood may be required.

Lifting veneers is a common problem, caused by shrinking, swelling or warping, degradation of glue, mould or insect attack under the veneer or a combination of these factors. It is important that loose veneer be relaid before it is damaged further or lost. Basically veneer is re-glued and pressed into place until set. It can be a complicated affair necessitating its removal, flattening, perhaps replacing missing parts and re-finishing. If the fault lies beneath the surface, this may have to be corrected.

Refinishing may be necessitated by re-pairs or spoiled surfaces. Obviously, it is best avoided as old patinas and antiquity can never be replaced. Good care should avoid the problem. Excess moisture causes French polish to bloom while alcohol removes the polish altogether. Finishes can be ruined by abrasion and blistered by heat.

Zealous attempts at cleaning away old wax and grime can go all the way through a perfectly sound and beautiful surface.

Always test any cleaning method first in an inconspicuous place. Old finishes have innumerable compositions and it can never be assumed that one cleaning method, no matter how well tried, will be foolproof for all jobs. One good cleaning solution can be made up of 2 parts white vinegar, 2 parts turpentine, 2 parts methylated spirits and 1 part linseed oil. Shake together well to form an emulsion and apply sparingly with cotton wool, changing the pad when soiled. This should remove old wax and grime, feed the polish and slightly soften it to form a new surface. It may be necessary to reduce the methylated spirit if it proves too strong on testing. Remember that some finishes are based on wax and a cleaner of this sort could remove the lot. This is not intended for repeated use.

To remove paint, use a solvent which leaves the original finish intact. Various organic solvents can be tried. All too often a paint stripper is the only solution and refinishing is necessary. Old and un-sightly varnishes may have to be treated in the same way. French polish can be removed with methylated spirits. The last residue of paint or varnish can be removed with wire wool, leaving a good surface to work with. Finishes can be removed by dipping in caustic soda solutions and this is done on a large scale. However, adhesives and joins are often degraded in the process.

New finishes should be in character with the period and original intention. Where possible the original type should be replaced. A certain expertise is required and a mess is likely without it. French polish and eboniz-ing are difficult. Varnishing can be easier. High gloss is usually lost on ageing so some matting down may be required. A fine abrasive, such as jeweller's rouge or a fine pumice powder rubbed on the surface with a soft brush gives a good final finish. Waxing helps to mellow, and has the added value of protecting the finish from excess moisture and abrasion. Wood is resilient but unless proper care is taken to ensure a reasonable environment, no amount of superficial attention can preserve it.

Charles Patterson
Conservation Officer, Horniman Museum

International Collections

U.S.A.	American Clock and Watch Museum, Bristol, Conn.	Clocks and Watches
	Boston Museum of Fine Arts, Boston, Mass.	Furniture, Ceramics, Glass, Silver, Oriental Art, Textiles
	Cincinnati Art Museum, Cincinnati.	Ceramics, Glass, Prints, Art Nouveau, Guns
	Cleveland Museum of Art, Cleveland, Ohio.	Oriental Art, Furniture, Guns
	Colonial Williamsburg, Williamsburg, Va.	Ceramics, Furniture, Textiles
	Corning Museum of Glass, New York, N.Y.	Glass
	Flint Institute of Art, Flint, Michigan.	Oriental Art, Glass
	Fogg Art Museum, Cambridge, Mass.	Oriental Art, Silver
	Freer Gallery of Art, Washington, D.C.	Oriental Art
	Frick Collection, New York, N.Y.	Furniture, Ceramics, Prints
	Henry Francis du Pont Winterthur Museum, Winterthur, Del.	Ceramics, Furniture, Textiles
	Mariners' Museum, Newport News, Virginia.	Maps, Prints
	Metropolitan Museum of Art, New York, N.Y.	Antiquities, Ceramics, Furniture, Jewelry, Oriental Art, Glass, Art Nouveau, Textiles, Silver
	New York University Museum of Clocks & Watches, New York, N.Y.	Clocks and Watches
	Philadelphia Museum of Art, Philadelphia, Pa.	Furniture, Glass, Silver
	Smithsonian Institution, Washington, D.C.	Ceramics, Glass, Silver, Guns, Clocks
	Stamford Historical Society, Stamford, Conn.	Textiles
	Textile Museum, Washington, D.C.	Textiles
	Wadsworth Atheneum, Hartford, Conn. (Colonel Samuel Colt Collection).	Guns
GREAT BRITAIN	American Museum in Britain, Claverton Manor, Bath.	Textiles, Furniture, Clocks, Silver
	Ashmolean Museum, Oxford.	Antiquities, Jewelry, Silver
	Bethnal Green Museum, London.	Art Nouveau
	British Museum, London.	Antiquities, Glass, Clocks, Maps & Prints, Guns
	City Museum and Art Gallery, Stoke.	Ceramics
	Goldsmiths' Company, London.	Silver and Gold
	Guildhall (Clockmakers' Company Collection), London.	Clocks
	Imperial War Museum, London.	Guns
	Percival David Foundation, London.	Oriental Art
	Pilkington Museum, St Helens.	Glass
	Science Museum, London.	Clocks
	Victoria and Albert Museum, London.	Ceramics, Glass, Furniture, Jewelry, Guns, Silver, Textiles, Maps & Prints, Oriental Art
	Wallace Collection, London.	Ceramics, Furniture
	William Morris Gallery, London.	Art Nouveau
EUROPE Austria	Heeresgeschichtliches Museum, Vienna.	Guns
France	Musée des Arts Décoratifs, Paris.	Antiquities, Ceramics, Furniture, Glass, Jewelry, Textiles, Silver, Gold, Clocks, Oriental Art
	Musée d'Ennery, Paris.	Oriental Art
	Musée du Louvre, Paris.	Antiquities, Ceramics, Clocks, Silver
	Musée National de Céramique, Sèvres.	Ceramics
	Musée National du Château de Versailles.	Furniture, Clocks
	Musée du Petit Palais, Paris.	Art Nouveau
Germany	Kunsthalle Bremen, Bremen.	Prints
	Staatliche Museen, Berlin.	Antiquities, Ceramics, Prints
The Netherlands	Rijksmuseum, Amsterdam.	Ceramics, Furniture, Silver, Glass
Norway	Kunstindustrimuseet i Oslo, Oslo.	Textiles, Ceramics, Glass, Furniture
Sweden	Nationalmuseum, Stockholm.	Antiquities, Prints

Index

Acknowledgments

Antique Dealer and Collectors Guide 4–5, 7 right, 92 below, 133; Antique Porcelain Co 4–5, 52; The American Museum, Bath 73; John Bethell 132–3; Blakemore 86; Boston Museum of Fine Arts 77; A. Brand/S. J. Phillips 40; Bristol Art Gallery 63 below; British Museum (John Freeman) 1, 4–5, 26, 27, 28, 29, 30, 32 below, 60 above, 92 above; F. N. Browning 120 above; Brooklyn Museum 36 below; Christie Manson and Woods 6, 44 below, 100, 101 above, 121, 124, 125, 139 above; Connaissance des Arts 51 below, 84 right, 87 right, 113; A. C. Cooper 8 left; Cooper Bridgeman front jacket, 4–5, 8 right, 33 above left, 33 below left, 37, 45, 49 below, 51 above, 90 left, 135 above, 143; Graham Dark 75 left; Michael Dyer Associates 84 left, 114 above, 145, 147 above, (Klingspor Museum, Offenbach); Editions Graphiques endpapers, 102 above, 102 below left; Eskenazi Ltd 139 below, 141; Werner Forman Archive 12, 13, 14, 15, 17 right, 19 below; Paul Forrester 2–3, 66 below; Douglas Gohm 23 above, 23 below, 24 above, 24 below, 25; Greenfield Village Collection and Henry Ford Museum, Dearborn, Michigan 91; Cecil Higgin Art Gallery 65; Hirmer Fotoarchiv, Munich 35 below, 35 right; Holbourne of Melstrie Museum 62; Michael Holford 18; Hong Kong City Museum and Art Galleries 134; Angelo Hornak 4–5, 7 left, 16 above, 54, 83 left, 90 right, 120 below, 129; Institute of Geological Sciences 104; John Jesse, London 53, 88; Jean Latham 112; Philippa Lewis 32 above; City of Liverpool Museum 61;

William MacQuitty 21; Malletts 78; Mansell Collection/Giraudon Louvre 10, 31, 138 below; Martins-Forrest Antiques, London 39, 150 above; Major Rudolf Mayer 89; Metropolitan Museum of Art 56, 81 above; Edwin Meyer, Vienna 119; Munchener Stadtmuseum 114 below; Musée des Arts Decoratifs 49 above; Collection of the William Nathaniel Banks 81 below; National Museum of Wales 52–53; National Trust (Clandon Park) 76 left; Meyrick Neilson 83 right, 85; New York, Museum of Modern Art 79; Parke Bernet Galleries, New York 4–5, 9 left, 38, 41, 43, 44 above; Perez London Ltd 4–5, 115 above, 115 below, 116, 117; S. J. Phillip 98–9; Philip and Sons, Cardiff 72; Museum of Industrial Art, Prague 67; Private Collection 68 left, 69, 122, 127 centre, 128; Royal Academy of Arts (Hendley Read Collection) 144; Royal Scottish Museum 60 below; Joseph Sataloff 4–5, 99 above, 99 below, 102 below right, 103; Scala 19 above, 36 above, 97; Smithsonian Institute 107, 108; Sotheby's 4–5, 9 right, 42, 47, 48, 64, 66 above, 87 left, 110, 123, 138; Spink and Son Ltd 140; City Museums, Stoke on Trent 16 below, 57; Tower of London Armouries 127 above, 127 below; Victoria and Albert Museum 50, 59, 93 left, 109, 110–111; Kenneth Ullyett 93 right; The Wallace Collection 95; Wartski Ltd 96, 105; Wedgwood and Sons 55; O. S. Wilson 76 right, 137; Henry Francis Dupont, Winterthur Museum 75 right; Roger Wood 17 left; ZEFA (E. Mariani) 13 below; Ziolo 4–5, 20, 33 right, 101 below, 147 below.

PDO 81-538